All White People Are Racist

Written By a White Man

Any sentence that starts with,
"I'm not racist, but..."
is racist.

Table of Contents

Forward to the Second Edition

When I released the first edition of this book, the political climate in Amerika was reaching yet another racial boiling point. This boiling point was certainly not the first we'd ever seen, nor will it be the last. It is also a boiling point that is perpetually on the brink of bubbling over at any given moment. Because that's what happens in a society built on and with racism. No matter how it's reformed or what new laws are enacted, there will always be racial tension brooding in the background waiting to explode. Until racism is uprooted from our society, there can never be peace, freedom, or justice for all. Because our society is the root of racism.

Due to the intensity of this racial tension, I was feeling a lot of self-imposed pressure to release this book. Not because I view myself as any kind of messiah or white hero. But because I felt that the political climate of the time was demanding any insightful value this book could possibly provide. The tension that was seething just beneath the surface of everyday life needed white people to gain some sense of perspective if we could ever hope for that tension to lead to a constructive outcome.

Contrary to the advice of those closest to me, I decided to release it anyway. Despite urging me to wait until I was absolutely certain that I was satisfied with the finished product, my anxiousness to release the book overtook the wise words of my partner and I released it. Who knew she'd be right!?

I wouldn't say that I instantly regretted the premature release of the first edition. Instead, the regret was actually more gradual as I had not yet realized that the book's release was, in fact, premature. However, the more I thought about the book, its content, and its relationship to the state of Amerika, as well as the world, the more it occurred to me that the book was not yet finished. Not only was the original book missing some very important key topics but, I also realized that I hadn't said everything I wanted to say, how I wanted to say it.

After this realization set in, over the following few months, I got to work expanding on the original text. Aside from editing and rephrasing some finer points here and there, I also added three more chapters. Additionally, I condensed one of the original chapters in with one of the new ones. As I continued to work on the book, some very high profile and controversial events took place that were directly related to the subject of the book including the Kyle Rittenhouse trial and subsequent acquittal in Wisconsin. The resurgence of the Chrystul Kizer murder trial and her self-defense case against her sex trafficker in the same city as Rittenhouse. The murder of Daunte Wright and Winston Smith in Minneapolis at the hands of police. The trial and subsequent conviction of Derrick Chauvin in the murder of George Floyd, also in Minneapolis. The trial and subsequent conviction of Gregory McMichael, Travis McMichael, and William Bryan who murdered Ahmaud Arbery while he was jogging through their neighborhood in Georgia. The last-minute commuted death penalty sentence for Julius Jones who is innocent of the crime for which he was convicted in Oklahoma. And the long overdue exoneration of Muhammad Aziz and Khalil Islam in the assassination of Malcolm X. It was seemingly endless. And all of this was going on as I was working to improve this book.

I started to feel even more pressure. I was feeling obligated to include some mention of all these different events that were happening at the same time that I was writing this book. I was driving myself crazy trying to keep notes and facts and all the information sorted. Then it hit me. It's always going to be that way. If I waited until no more newsworthy racial issues occurred so that I could include them all to release the book, the book would never be complete. There will always be controversial and notable events occurring in which race antagonisms play a part. As long as Amerika and the systems of society, politics and economics on which it functions still stands as we know it, there will be high profile, highly publicized racist events. And the fact that I'm able to sit here and provide so many contemporary examples is argument enough for the validity and veracity of that claim and consequently, this book. So, it was that I decided to refine what I had already written in the first edition, added in the more general, common and prevalent issues not yet mentioned the first time, and release a second edition.

Nevertheless, although I do not feel the need to expand on every single socio-political event that has occurred involving race antagonisms while writing this book, I would like to point out a few things regarding the Rittenhouse trial. In the aftermath of his acquittal, Kyle Rittenhouse was, of course, inundated with interview after interview. He was thrust into the public eye as a modern spokesperson for violent provocation disguised as selective self-defense, palatable racism, and white pathology. The spin that his public relations managers and agents chose to place on his position was one that, while still a thin veil for his white supremacist mentality, also one that sought to appeal to both conservatives and liberals alike. In one of the more notable interviews on FOXNews, Kyle Rittenhouse mentions to Tucker Carlson that he's not racist and that he supports BLM. I'm not going to argue whether he is or not racist. I think that crossing state lines with a high-powered rifle that you're not legally supposed to have under the age of 18 to protect a business that isn't even yours, killing 2 BLM protesters, injuring a 3rd, and then taking pictures and drinking beers with members of a reputed white nationalist organization like the Proud Boys while awaiting trial for the aforementioned murders are actions that speak for themselves. What I would like to point out, however, is the comments that Tucker Carlson made about Rittenhouse following his interview with him. Carlson portrays Rittenhouse as a hero, almost like a good Samaritan. He says Rittenhouse struck him as "bright, decent, sincere, dutiful, and hardworking" and later, "a sweet kid". However, Carlson then goes on to say that Rittenhouse "isn't especially political". Aside from any number of questions and contradictions this last statement raises, it also struck me as evidence to support an important point.

Racism is a construct that spans all 3 major pillars of a functioning society. The social, economic and political. In the Jim Crow south, there were laws that mandated segregation. These laws made for some egregious living, social, and working conditions for Black people. During chattel slavery, the slave codes were written into the laws making it legal for private citizens to own slaves and amass a fortune from the forced labor of the enslaved people. When a cop murders a Black person and is acquitted of that murder based on the laws that protect the cop's actions, it is in a political sphere that this occurs. Racism exists within a political spectrum on which everyone who participates in society takes a stance whether they consciously choose to or not. This is because racism is woven into the fabric of our society. Therefore, politically ignorant people who take action in politically charged conflicts where there is an imbalance of power, are destined to end up on the side that seeks to maintain the unequal power balance. Be it by choice or by default, political action through political ignorance will always end up supporting the wrong side of history. It is specifically because Kyle Rittenhouse was not "especially political" that he ended up where he did. And that's how racism works. Racism uses its power to control others. Whether it is controlling us by force or by conditioning is situational. But either way, racism controls everyone who lives within the society in which racism is present and places them on either one side of it or the other. In a world where the concept of race among humans even exists, lacking a political consciousness is enough to automatically place you on the side of pro-racism. It is this ignorance that I'm hoping to extinguish and consciousness that I'm seeking to spark.

<u>All White People Are Racist</u>

<u>Preface</u>

Gloria Steinem said, "The truth shall set you free, but first it'll piss you off". I think it's safe to say that this book is bound to upset a lot of people, mostly white. But that's not the reason for writing it, however. I don't seek to intentionally ruffle anyone's feathers. I don't subscribe to the notion that inflammatory commentary or personal attacks are a necessary contribution to relevant political discourse. Nevertheless, considering the nature of this topic, I think it's pretty obvious that the controversy is bound to rile some emotions that white people have regarding the subject.

My hope is that at least some people will have enough maturity and self-awareness to realize that their anger or resentment towards this book is a product of being offended by it. And being offended means having hurt feelings. I hope some people will be able to see past their own hurt feelings and realize there's a deeper and more important issue which needs to be addressed. If not, well then you're still just too afraid to admit that you got your feelings hurt by a book title.

There were a few people who suggested that I soften the title of the book in order to gain more readership. I emphatically declined for two reasons. One, as white people, we really need to learn to get over ourselves, stop being so emotionally weak, and desist placing more importance on our own hurt feelings than on other peoples' lives. And two, because I believe it's time to pick a side. The days of riding the fence, avoiding the issue, and playing arbiter are over. No longer can society afford white people the luxury of burying our heads in the sand. To do so literally costs people their lives. I sincerely believe that there are at least some white people whose sense of social responsibility and outrage at injustice are strong enough to override their sensitivity to being faced with their own racism enough to compel their own self-reflection and attitude adjustments. I firmly maintain that we as white people are collectively capable of doing better. My faith in humanity necessitates my belief that we are able to grow and evolve past our current arrogance and denial of a social malfeasance that our ancestors created.

Of course, not everyone is going to be convinced. It would be naïve to think that every white person in the world is socially responsible and intellectually inclined enough to consider – or even care - that our collective understanding of racism, what constitutes it, and how it works has been grossly distorted. Pointing out the irony in being the ones who invented racism (slavery based on the ideology that skin color and culture determine the social status and consideration of one's humanity, as well as every other socio-economic arrangement that has followed since) yet having very little understanding of how it works is going to make quite a few people who are just not emotionally or intellectually equipped to face it very defensive and combative. And that's just the way it goes. The people who so ardently advocate for personal responsibility do so because they don't want to take social responsibility. Social responsibility requires caring about something and someone other than yourself. Caring about someone besides yourself means you have to take the risk of something or someone not caring for you in return. That's a frightening prospect when you've been hurt by things you used to care about, which is so often the case with people who walk around wearing apathy as a virtue. This is why it's weak to use it as an excuse to avoid doing the right thing. And when you're not ready to take responsibility, being held accountable will feel like an attack. Again, the irony.

Still, I find it necessary to write this book because history has determined it to be socially imperative. Almost everyone will agree that racism is bad and must be eliminated. But few are able to agree on what racism is. Creating campaigns and social movements that seek to eliminate racism without a clear mutual understanding of it and how it works only allows for its continuation. By reason of vague interpretation followed by incorrect assumptions, people will agree to combat racism without agreeing on how to identify it. If I understand racism to be a thing that's bad and you understand racism is something else that's bad but, these two understandings do not match each other, then our interpretations of racism do not align. If our interpretations of racism do not align with each other, then every action that follows will be contradictory and we will end up working against each other. Those who were supposed to be an ally become an obstacle. If we want to create movements and campaigns that fight racism, we must first communicate with each other in order to clarify our own understanding of racism. Then we need to be willing to be wrong. We have to allow ourselves the room for that understanding to be adjustable. In order for our understanding of racism to become mutual with others, we need to understand that, as white people, we do not get to determine what racism is. And I say that as a white man writing this book. Because everything I write about racism in this book I was first taught by Black people.

The bottom line, however, is that whether or not we accept that racism still exists or have any interest in eradicating it, white people need to collectively come to grips with the reality that a society created on inequality and oppression cannot bare the fruit of freedom, justice, and democracy. You see, even if you believe everything you've been taught in school - exactly the way it's been taught - there's no denying that Amerika was founded on the backs of slavery and genocide. Slavery and genocide that used the idea of race as the basis for its motivating force. The arrogant notion that Native and Black people were backward savages, culturally uncivilized, and destined for a life of bondage and subjugation to white people is precisely the same thought process that seeps into our subconscious and influences our approach to life, relationships, and society to this day. In one form or another the biases held about Black, Brown, Native, and Asian people that were prevalent when this country was being built are woven into the ideas that set the foundation for its construction. So obviously we are not responsible for its creation. But we are responsible for its destruction. Despite the current prevailing attitude towards the matter, we are, in fact, responsible for the choices our ancestors made, just like our children will be responsible for the choices that we make. Therein lies our personal relationship to social responsibility.

If we have any interest whatsoever in a society free from racism, we must first understand it. If we do not understand how something works, how can we attempt to effectively fight it? How will we know how to recognize when it is present? How will we know if and when we have even defeated it, for that matter...? Understanding racism on a level that is deeper than what the society that created it allows us to is the first step in eliminating it.

In order for us to gain a better understanding, we must first be willing to separate ourselves from the current one we hold. As white people in a society such as ours, we cannot help but have beliefs and attitudes that are shaped by the world we live in. When the world we live in was built with and on racism, it is inevitable that some of our thought patterns, attitudes, and beliefs will be shaped by it.

Because our psyche is influenced by our environment and our environment is built on social structures that were molded by white supremacy, we must also understand that the world we live in is perceived and experienced very differently than the way others experience and perceive it. A failure to acknowledge that is to suggest two things. 1) that everything about the world we live in is correct. And 2) that everyone else's world is exactly the same as ours. Neither of these implications are accurate for obvious reasons. They are both narrow minded and naive assumptions that no reasonable person would conclude. If we can understand that people in different countries have a different experience in the world than we do simply by virtue of a difference in environment, then surely, we can understand that people with different skin color also have a different world experience than us by reason of a difference in environment. The world environment that Black, Brown, and Native people are subjected to is much different than the one we as white people are subjected to. Simply by way of treatment, assumption, and bias, Black people can be standing a mere five feet away from a white person and still be in a completely different environment. Based on the treatment they receive, and the assumptions being made about them, all through biases that are either indoctrinated into the people within their proximity or embedded into our social composition, or both, Black, Brown, Native, and Asian people automatically endure a different environment than we do. The details of just how different our environments are will be explained throughout the book.

Nevertheless, we need to be willing to detach ourselves from our current perspective so that we can consider new ones. In order for us to understand these differences and grasp their extremes, we need to be willing to consider that our lives could be very different if we were born under different circumstances and that these different circumstances would change how we see the world. We would never be able to put ourselves in Black, Brown, or Native people's shoes when it comes to world experience. But that doesn't mean we can't see their perspective. We just have to be willing to.

The psychological phenomenon known as cognitive complexity describes a person's ability to recognize that two or more perspectives can be valid at the same time. This comes from the understanding that each person's world view is shaped by their life experiences and that each person's experiences are different. It's time for white people to gain some cognitive complexity and understand that the world we live in is not the same for everyone else. Our life experiences are not the same as everyone else.

There is another psychological phenomenon known as cognitive dissonance. Cognitive dissonance is a contradiction to cognitive complexity however, ironically, its contradiction works in a very similar way to cognitive complexity. Cognitive dissonance is the state of having two or more conflicting or inconsistent beliefs simultaneously. As humans, we have a tendency to develop strong emotional attachments to our beliefs. When faced with new information that challenges, disproves, or otherwise invalidates these beliefs, these emotional attachments generally tend to cause the rejection or denial of this new information in order to hang onto our current beliefs. Avoiding the discomfort that accompanies cognitive dissonance is prioritized over facing the discomfort that accompanies an update to our beliefs. Holding onto certain attitudes or beliefs in the face of facts that disprove them is delusional and arrogant. It's also about the most Amerikan thing one can do.

With all of that said, I feel it pertinent to clarify that I have no interest in changing people's minds. That's not what this book is about. Banging my head against a wall trying to convince people of their own racism when they so obviously have an emotional commitment to denying it is just as ignorant and pointless as racism itself. Some people are so evolved and developed that they do not need to self-reflect or reconsider what they believe. They don't have a racist bone in their body. There are other people who are so smart and so educated that there isn't possibly anything more they could learn about racism. And because they know every single thing there is to know about racism, they know every single way there is to not be racist. Both of these types of people are committed to their own ignorance. Trying to educate someone who is committed to their own ignorance is an exercise in futility that I have no time or energy for. Arguing with the village idiot begs the question, "who's who?"

However, those of us white people with any semblance of interest in improving our society and progressing humanity, must separate ourselves from our contemporary thought process, if even only temporarily, so that we can at least consider the possibility that other valid perspectives exist. We have to be willing to develop cognitive complexity and see that ours is not the only valid world view. In fact, for some of us, we have to be willing to consider that our world view is just flat out wrong. Finally, we have to be aware of our propensity for cognitive dissonance. Staring in the face of facts we don't like can be scary and intimidating. Holding onto beliefs in the face of facts that disprove them because it's too scary to change what we believe is weak. Don't be weak. I'm simply asking the skeptical and defensive white people to suspend your skepticism and defense until you've read through the book. Give it a chance. Just consider for a moment that we do not, in fact, know it all. We are human. As such, there will be times that we will be mistaken. We have to be willing to learn and consider that we could very well do better than what we currently are doing. Just for a minute, try to consider that, despite all the rhetoric we're subjected to, there is actually quite a lot we could learn from Black people.

Introduction

Dr Martin Luther King, Jr once said, "Whites, it must frankly be said, are not putting in a similar mass effort to reeducate themselves out of their racial ignorance. It is an aspect of their sense of superiority that the white people of America believe they have so little to learn." The problem with white children learning about racism from public education is that the school curriculum and the western concept of education as a whole was created by and for white people. Therefore, school is a white supremacist institution. The way racism is taught in school is a very one-dimensional perspective with a lot of false implications and misinterpretations attached. As such, our society has produced generation after generation of children growing into adults who will do anything to keep from being called racist except not be racist. We are fine with being racist as long as people don't think we're racist. The minute our racism is exposed, we exert more energy denying our racism than we do to correct it. We use every tactic and excuse in the book. From "I have friends that are Black" to the ridiculous and fallacious concept of "reverse racism" to justify, deny, and deflect our racist tendencies.

One of the most misunderstood aspects of racism is that it is both durable and dynamic. Racism adjusts itself to be compatible with the times. This is because, contrary to popular white belief, racism is not based on the idea of a love/hate paradigm. Hate is an expression of racism. One of the many different available expressions of it. But it is not a requirement for it. Because, again, contrary to popular white belief, racism doesn't just look like white hoods and burning crosses. It can also appear friendly or considerate because racism doesn't just target skin color, it also targets culture. It can just as easily be expressed by fetishizing Black bodies and putting dreadlocks in our hair. White people who exclusively date people of another race are demonstrating yet another latent form of racism. We've either reduced the value of our preferred counterpart down to a sexual fetish or we're using them to try and disprove our own racism. In either instance, the humanity and equal status of the other race is dissolved.

In most cases, our motives are so ingrained and subconscious that we're bereft of the realization that we even do this. Most people who are racist have no idea that they're racist. The genocidal nature of overt racism is actually the minority of racists. These days, most white people are so pressed to prove we aren't racist that our efforts to do so only end up highlighting our racism. Racism is, in fact, based on the idea of an inferior/superior paradigm. You can love a dog and still treat it like it's inferior to you. But you can only treat the dog like it's inferior to you because you have the power to do so. With all that being said, it is important to keep five fundamental concepts in mind throughout the course of this book:

- **Racism requires power.**

Capitalism is where racism gets its power from. Chattel slavery was the scientific means through which capitalism was instituted into society. Effectively, the slave trade was the capital for capitalism. This is why you cannot have capitalism without racism. Racism is prejudice and/or discrimination with the power to enforce it thereby affecting the everyday lives of an entire race. Because Black people were the enslaved race, they have been systematically barred from gaining any institutional power. Without power, there is no way to collectively enforce the prejudices, biases and attitudes on other people.

- **The aforementioned definition of racism is also why reverse racism does not exist.**

Prejudice and discrimination are not the same as racism. Black people can be prejudice and they discriminate. But they cannot be racist. The prejudice and degrading attitudes and beliefs that white people hold and express, whether we realize it or not, are most often times either adopted or evolved from the attitudes and beliefs that were widely held by white people while constructing the society we live in today. Therefore, when we hold or express these attitudes and beliefs, they are merely a reflection of those that are embedded within the social, political, and economic institutions on which our society functions. The suggestion or belief that reverse racism exists is to suggest or believe that Jewish people had just as much power to oppress the Nazis as the Nazis did the Jews. This is why no one can be racist against white people. Not even other white people.

- **Integration did not mean equality.**

In order for integration to equal equality, the system that Black people were integrated into would first have had to be equal. Black people were integrated into an unequal system and placed at the bottom of it. By affirming the integration of Black, Brown, and Native people into the society that was designed by white people, we are suggesting that not only do we know how to construct society better than Black, Brown, and Native people but, we are also implying that we know what is best for them and that it is our society that is what's best for them. What happened last time white people thought we knew what was best Black and Native people?

- **The white savior complex is racism on the other end of the racist spectrum**

It is an expression of racism manifested through endeavors like missionary work, international litigious processes, and the nonprofit industry. It is based on the idea that Black people and other people of color lack sufficient ability to solve their own problems and ameliorate their own circumstances, so they need white people to do it for them. There's nothing wrong with trying to make a difference in the world. But using Black suffering to make yourself feel relevant and better about yourself is also racist because it does these things by appealing to your ego thereby making you feel superior.

- **We need to stop trying to use the dictionary definitions of racism to try and justify reverse racism.**

Dictionaries are written by universities that are part of the education system. As previously elucidated, the education system is a white supremacist institution. Ergo, dictionary definitions are created by white people. Allowing white people to define racism is like allowing sex offenders to define rape.

We need to understand how complex and dynamic racism really is. Our racism is just as predominant and obvious in the white savior complex as it is in lynching black men.

Now that these 5 points have been clarified, let me just end by saying a few words. First, I admittedly did not cover the topics of anti-Brown, anti-Native or anti-Asian racism nearly as much as anti-Black racism. Due to the nature of race relations and their historical overview in this country, and indeed, the world, I felt that the severity of anti-Black racism which continues to emanate from Amerika and pollute the minds and perspectives of the rest of the world required an emphasis on the Black question. However, I would like to recognize and acknowledge the struggle against white supremacy that is faced by Brown, Native, and Asian people as well. The way this struggle plays out in their respective communities may be different but, the cause is the same.

Secondly, I don't care about how offended you are by the book or its title. Toughen up snowflake. Stop making everything about you. Your feelings are not more important than putting an end to racism. White tears and self-righteous indignation are just a manifestation of white guilt, which is unproductive and selfish. Lastly, we live in the age of information. If you're skeptical or mad that I didn't use citations, oh well. The evidence to corroborate what I state is right at your fingertips. Google it. There's only one reason you would choose not to, and there's an entire chapter on that later in the book.

Chapter 1
White Supremacy and Amerikanization

When we hear the term white supremacy, we tend to think of Nazi Germany along with the extreme environment and conditions that ensued under Nazi rule. While fascism is indeed white supremacy, it's not the only way white supremacy manifests. If we think about what the phrase "white supremacy" means at its core, we can agree that, essentially, it means the dominant functions of society are established by white people, for white people, under the idea that those functions are what's best for society as a whole.

Any society that is constructed and developed by the white way of doing things is white supremacist. What do I mean by the "white way"? It is the way in which white people decided is the correct way to do things. For example, it was white people who decided that education has to look like a teacher standing in front of a room full of students sitting in uniform desks while listening to and memorizing facts. It was white people who decided that prisons and slavery were an appropriate response to crime. It was white people who decided what constitutes crime. It was white people who decided that police were an acceptable institution for social control. It was white people who decided that capitalism would be the best economic arrangement.

So, a white supremacist society is any society where the white way of doing things is not only the dominant way of doing things but one that favors white people over everyone else. This is where the idea of white privilege comes from. The circumstance of white privilege is a byproduct that comes from the white people who arranged society to benefit them at the expense of others. Mainly people with different skin color and different economic status. Often times those two are one and the same.

With this understanding of context, it's important to further understand how a white supremacist society is maintained. How it perpetuates itself. In 1933 Dr Carter G Woodson published a book called "The Miseducation of the Negro." In it, Woodson discusses how Black people in the Amerikan school system are not being educated as much as they are being culturally indoctrinated. Essentially, they are being Americanized. However, the miseducation of the negro also resulted in the miseducation of white people. Because we are also subjected to the same curriculum, so too are we also Americanized. The curriculum that teaches Black people to love the Amerikan way of doing things, and thus, be content with a life of subjugation, is the same one that teaches us to love the Amerikan way of doing things and thus, be content with a life of privilege. Privilege at the expense of others' subjugation. It's the same one that teaches us to believe that the Amerikan way of doing things is the right way of doing things and that this way of doing things is what equals freedom. This means that from birth, we are socialized and conditioned to be racist. Because a handful of rich white slave owning, genocidal men decided that they knew best how to create a society that was free, equal, and just. Naturally, however, the society they wanted to create would sustain the lifestyle to which they had become accustomed. The lifestyle of stealing land, mass murdering the people that land belongs to, enslaving people, brutalizing them, terrorizing them, dehumanizing them and exploiting their labor.

This is what makes Amerika just as white supremacist as Nazi Germany. Because that is the same society that we still live in today. The society we live in today was built with the brutality and arrogance of white supremacist ideology. In fact, in Mien Kampf, Hitler admits to using the Amerikan government's treatment of the natives and Black people as a blueprint for what he would do to Jewish people. It is these sentiments that are the foundation for every popular belief and attitude that white people in Amerika hold towards Black people, native people, brown people, poor people, and anyone else who does not conform to the ideal Amerikan way of doing things. Because racism doesn't just target skin color. It also targets culture.

And any culture that is practiced and/or developed by any people of color will inevitably deviate from the Amerikan way of doing things because the Amerikan way of doing things was developed by white Europeans. This is precisely why Amerika is not officially opposed to immigrants. Most Amerikans will tell you that they don't have a problem with people from other countries coming here as long as they do it "the right way". What most people won't tell you is what they mean by "the right way". The so-called "right way" implies more than just following the legal channels to citizenship. It also implies the requirement of assimilation to the Amerikan way of life. If you're willing to follow the laws that were set up by people who came here in the same manner and under the same pretenses that you did, surrender to our way of life, and establish a firm belief in that way of life, then you can live in Amerika. Of course we cannot promise that you will be treated the same as white people. Whether they were born here or they emigrated from Europe, white people will be given preferential treatment. However, you can still live here and glorify Amerika while we bomb your country back to the stone age and economically rape it for all its natural resources.

As white people with a strong emotional investment in the Amerikan way of doing things, we have a tendency to degrade, chastise, alienate, and deride any other way of doing things that does not coincide or match with the Amerikan way. This strong emotional investment comes from years of indoctrination; of conditioning towards the patriotism that allows Amerikan white supremacy to perpetuate itself. As a result of this conditioning, over time, we develop attitudes from which things like "if he would have just followed orders, the cop wouldn't have shot him", "hip hop leads to violence", "if he pulled his pants up and turned his music down, the cops wouldn't have profiled him", "Use proper English", "use proper grammar", etc are derived. And because these attitudes and beliefs aren't necessarily entrenched in hate for the people, most people who are racist have no idea that they are racist. Instead, these attitudes and beliefs drive us to construct counter movements solely to shut down Black people's struggle for liberation like All Lives Matter and Blue Lives Matter. We don't do it necessarily to deny the validity of Black lives. We do it because of our sensitivity to being excluded from the spotlight. For centuries, society has been focused on appeasing and catering to white people. Particularly white men. We have been the center of social attention and praise for so long that the minute a movement gains international attention that isn't about stroking our egos, we throw adult temper tantrums. White people, particularly white men, are so spoiled that if anything isn't about us, we have to go and make it about us. All of a sudden kneeling during the national anthem is disrespectful to soldiers. Soldiers who fight for Amerikan imperialism. Hint: it was never about soldiers or military in the first place. We are spoiled and thus feel attacked. All of this feels like a personal attack on white people because our entire identity has been built on racism; on the degradation and subjugation of people with different skin colors and cultures in order to make ourselves feel worthy, feel valid. Racism is the foundation of white identity. Furthermore, the perpetuation of white identity is maintained through a concerted effort not just within confines Amerika's borders but, global indoctrination towards an Amerikan monoculture as well. The white supremacist conditioning of Americanization is not a phenomenon that is experienced solely within the limits of the United States. It is also asserted on a global scale. Perhaps more aggressively even.

Bill Nye once said that Amerika's largest export, for better or for worse, is culture. He wasn't necessarily referring to sacred rites, ancient practices, and artistic expression influenced by life within a particular social arrangement. I believe Bill Nye was talking more about the attitudes and beliefs that Amerika thrusts about itself onto the rest of the world through its very powerful propagandist strength. This propaganda is enforced through Amerika's economic and military strength. It is then reinforced through the commercialism and consumerism of fast-food chains, designer brand clothing, Eurocentric standards of beauty, and mass media. All leading to the indoctrination of false conceptions about the Amerikan social, economic and political climate. Since its inception, Amerika has propagated itself as the "land of the free, home of the brave". It champions itself as the "land of opportunity". However, what fails to get propagated is the glaring class dichotomy intersecting with the overt race antagonism that sprung up the minute white people decide to take this land for ourselves and force Black people to build white society for free through the most brutal, barbaric, and terrorizing form of slavery the world has ever seen. The society that was built off the backs and lives of Black people has now evolved (if you could even call it that) into one that A) has yet to abolish slavery B) sees the largest prison population not just globally but historically as well which, despite being only 14% of the population, is over 65% Black C) has 6 empty houses to every one homeless person, and D) has over 16 million children that go to bed hungry every night. In addition, the U.S. is where, again, despite being only 14% of the population, Black people are 2.5 times more likely to be murdered by police than the white people who make up over 70% of the population. What Amerika didn't tell the rest of the world is that even if it is the "land of opportunity", it is not the land of *equal* opportunity. The system on which Amerikan society was built is based on inequality. Insofar as this is the same system on which Amerika functions today, it couldn't possibly have equal opportunity for everyone. Therefore, since these aspects of Amerikan society don't get nearly as much global recognition as the alternate propagandized aspects - despite being the more accurate of the two - the world began to take on a very different conception of what Amerika has to offer than what the reality actually is. And because the world viewed Amerika in a light that was grossly inaccurate, it started to believe that the aforementioned white Amerikan way of constructing a society, and all the beliefs and attitudes that go along with it, was superior to any other way. Large portions of the entire world started to become Amerikanized without even living in Amerika.

The result of all this is the value that other people in other countries place on their own culture gets overridden by the value they are being conditioned to place on Amerikan culture. Because that's what racism does. It doesn't just target skin color; it also targets the cultures of people with different skin color. So even if All Lives Matter wasn't a blatant attempt to tell Black people "stay-in-your-place", it's still racist because it's an argument against Black people's call for help which is attempting to shut Black people up. What white people need to understand is that not all of our racist attitudes and beliefs were a conscious decision. Some of them were planted in our subconscious long before we even knew what race was. Yet, although we may not be responsible for developing them, we are responsible for changing them. We still have to separate ourselves from the emotional investment we have in the tenets we live by. Then make an objective analysis on our attitudes and beliefs. And change or eliminate any of them that are rooted in the subjection, degradation, or subordination of others. It is not more noble to deny our racism than it is to acknowledge and fix it. Fixing our own racist beliefs is more anti-racist than trying to convince the world that we're not racist.

Chapter 2
Fetishism

Racism is so ingrained into Amerikan culture that even our attempts to prove we're not racist end up highlighting our racism. Nowhere else is this more apparent than the attitude of fetishism that is developed out of cultural indoctrination. What exactly is fetishism? Fetishism is the acute and exclusive sexual attraction to anyone of a different race based solely on the stereotypical features and characteristics of said race. In other words, fetishism is the sexual objectification of an entire race. It should be noted that there is a distinction between being physically at-tracted to certain features or characteristics typically associated with a certain race and reducing someone's worth down to a sexual attraction exclusively because of those features or characteristics. This is why when white men/women say, "I love Black/Latina/Asian men/women", it is still a statement replete with racist undertones. Nevertheless, fetishism is a very complex phenomenon in itself due to both its roots and its evolution over time.

During chattel slavery, it wasn't unheard of for slave masters to have their way with enslaved women at any time they felt like it. Often times, enslaved women were given as "gifts" to certain men of the house spe-cifically for this purpose. Despite being considered only 3/5 of a human being, it was very common for enslaved Black women to bear the children of the white slave owners. (Incidentally, this speaks volumes to the pathological mindset that is necessary to own slaves). The phenomenon of fetishism developed due to the over sexualization of Black women by white men as well as the portrayal of the sexual savagery of Black men by white women.

In the case of Black women, their naturally curvaceous bodies became associated with the assumption of an insatiable sexual prowess that was able to give white men a sexual experience that white women just could not. This fetishization evolved into the reduction of Black women as nothing more than sex objects. Even after chattel slavery was abolished, the stereotype stuck. Today, there are hordes of white men who think that their sexual attraction to Black women solely for their bodies and the perception of unparalleled sexual satisfaction excludes them from being racist. The irony being, that their attraction is itself racist due to its disregard for anything else that makes Black women human.

In the case of Black men, they are also reduced down to the stereotype of their anatomy by white women. Most white women who exclusively date Black men, do so while often subconsciously subscribing to the stereotype of an uncivilized, savage "mandingo" who is unable to control his sexual urges. A stereotype which has stuck with Black men since they were first falsely accused and executed for raping white women. This stereotype is very similar to that of Black women in that it projects Black men to be more well-endowed and more uninhibited in bed than white men which will inevitably give white women a sexual experience that white men just cannot match. This racist development was born out of the idea that Black men are so savage that they are unable to control their sexual urges. This led to the belief that if left unsupervised, they would inevitably rape white women due to their uncontrollable sexual attraction to them. This ridiculous notion left a number of glaring errors in the undue arrogance of the white mentality, not the least of which was the idea that white women set the standard for beauty and attraction. Still, this mentality evolved and progressed in the minds of white women who got such an adrenaline rush from the feeling of being desired by some exotic, hypersexualized creature that their curiosity, along with their libido, was piqued. The rise of this stereotype created a very convenient opportunity for modern white women who now believe that their fetish with Black men not only absolves them of their racism, but that it also gives them access to the Black community. Both of which are also racist beliefs.

Furthermore, this fetishization also provided the opportunity for white men to exercise both state sanctioned as well as extrajudicial lynchings en mass in the name of "justice" for white women who falsely accused Black men of rape (enter Emit Till, the Scottsboro boys, the Central Park Five, et al). However, it should be stated and understood that the real reason these lynchings occurred was to satisfy white men's jealousy for their perceived sexual inadequacy and racism projected by hate for their deep-seated feelings of inferiority disguised as perceived superiority.

Much the same things can be said when predominantly white men narrow their romantic focus to Latina women or Asian women. Latinas have a stereotypical reputation for being "fiery", aggressive, and feisty. Asian women have a stereotypical reputation for being submissive, passive, and docile. White men perceive these stereotypes as the basis for both their ideological romantic relationship as well as a sexual experience that white women are unable to provide. White women who fetishize Latin or Asian men will often do so on a similar stereotypical basis. Latin men are generally thought to be passionate and overly sexual while Asian men are thought to be rational, loyal, and, secure. Both white men and white women who fetishize a particular race will seek out relationships based on these stereotypes in order to fulfill the fetish that is aroused by them while almost completely overlooking anything else that makes them human.

If you are white and your partner is not free to be Black, Brown, Asian or Indigenous without incurring some form of push back or opposition from you, then chances are, you're only in that relationship because you fetishize the other person. This makes you racist as well.

As previously mentioned, fetishism does not absolve racism. It accentuates it. Personally, I don't believe there is anything wrong with interracial relationships. I'm in one myself. However, if you are white and you exclusively only date one particular race, that makes you racist because reducing your own sexual attraction down to a stereotype is racist. It is racist because it objectifies everyone of that race solely for sexual satisfaction. It then simultaneously and automatically reduces everyone else of that race down to that stereotype and removes every other complexity that makes everyone of that race a complete human being.

This is unless, of course, you exclusively only date white people. To do this implies either negligence to recognize worth and beauty in any other race, or implies some bias held against the entire race. The aforementioned bias is usually based on one of two things. Either a negative personal experience that was had in the past led to the development of this bias and the application of it to everyone of that race, or a belief in the generalized personality trait stereotypes that come along with vilifying an entire race (e.g. "all Black men are dogs" "all Black women are gold diggers" "all Latino men are hot headed" etc.). Either way is a degradation of everyone categorized by that race.

Fetishism also extends beyond just intimate relationships and sexual attraction. Exotifying mixed children goes along with fetishism as well. The aesthetics of mixed children is an attraction that stems from a conception of beauty that prioritize appearances resembling traditional European features. Lighter colored eyes, thinner curly hair, pointier nose, and thinner lip lines all blended into a human with a skin color that's darker but not "too dark" is a fetish that holds beauty in a light standardized by whiteness. Children are only considered aesthetically pleasing if they're mixed with white.

The other side of this mentality is that society is only able to have a standard of beauty if it also has a standard of ugly with which to compare and contrast appearances with. Guess which appearances are used to accomplish this. Yeah, darker skin, wider nose, thicker lips, kinkier course hair. You know, anything that doesn't indicate mixing with European blood. Now imagine little boys and girls whose features match this description and the self-image it creates. What impact do you think this has on little boys and girls who have hearts filled with love, but heads filled self-hate. Imagine your child, or even yourself, growing up with a daily increase in negative self-image and a decrease in self-esteem.

This raises an issue in the Black community known as colorism. Basically, colorism is the conflict between light and dark skin, as well as the features typically associated with each one respectively and which one constitutes beauty. However, being a white man, it is not my place to speak on colorism. Nor is going in depth on the topic relevant to this book. What I will say however, is that if it weren't for white supremacy and the conditioning of beauty standards that necessarily accompany it in the west, there would be no issue of colorism in the Black community.

Nevertheless, it still remains that this narrow concept of beauty persists. And it is a beauty standard that is further upheld by capitalism. Deciding which features and appearances in children are marketable is a decision that comes down to what society deems to be preferential in the real world. This preference is guided by European beauty standards. Once society has chosen which features it prefers, advertising and media then preys on these preferences by overexposing their portrayal of them. This, in turn, not only increases the profits of media and advertising companies but, also serves to reinforce what society considers to be beautiful. It is a vicious cycle that preys on innocent children.

Yet, due to our gross misunderstanding of racism, fetishization is just another form of racism that we as white people often mistake for exemption from it. Contrary to popular Eurocentric belief, when we fetishize people of other races, we are just as guilty of racism as if we had burned a cross on their front lawn or locked them up in concentration camps.

Chapter 3
Integration Does Not Mean Equality

This chapter requires a short preface for a disclaimer. The reader should be aware that this chapter seemingly goes astray from the overall topic. However, this little detour is done intentionally to provide context for the chapter and by the end, we will see that it has come full circle back to the original topic at hand with all the pieces connected.

For starters, since we have such a strong propensity to cherry pick Dr. Martin Luther King, Jr's quotes to try and deny, disguise, or justify our racism by taking them out of context and regurgitating them mid-argument, it would probably be wise to look at some of his other, lesser-known quotes that cannot be misunderstood in any context to compare them to the ones that are all too often cited by white people to refute our racism. Clarifying his actual position on the subjects of racism, integration, and capitalism is bound to confuse a lot of white people. What his actual views were are going challenge and conflict with some of our previous understandings of what we thought they were. After these mis-understandings are clarified, we need to reassess whether or not we still agree with him. Considering the conflicts in our beliefs that are sure to arise in light of these new understandings we have to ask ourselves, are we prepared to be just as vocal and public about disagreeing with Martin

Luther King, Jr as we were when we agreed with him? If so, are we prepared to take on the social considerations that disagreeing with Rev. Dr. Martin Luther King, Jr implies?

When Martin Luther King, Jr. said, "I fear I may have integrated my people into a burning house." It was a denunciation of the Amerikan way. Hence, the fear. Subsequently, the previously mentioned "Americanization" and cultural indoctrination of this burning house has bred generation after generation of people who believe that the so-called Amerikan way of life is the epitome of freedom and democracy. Without questioning the validity of this claim by examining any of the evidence we have been given to support it, this idea will inevitably lead us to believe that anyone who is included in our society has the same rights, freedoms, and privileges that are professed to come along with being the so-called freest society in the world. This is precisely why some believe that Amerika is a post-racial society. The people who buy into the Americanization that they are inundated with have a very distorted understanding of how racism manifests in the everyday life of society. By believing that the way our society functions is the pinnacle of freedom and democracy, we develop the false assumption that integration into said society guaranteed the same for Black people. It didn't. And it didn't because it couldn't. It couldn't because, despite all the patriotic claims, Amerikan chauvinism, and a presumption of superiority through distorted comparisons to other countries, Amerikan society is not, in fact, the best way to organize a society. How could a country with the highest rate of imprisonment in the world have the best answer to crime? How could a country where student loan debt exceeds all other debt have the best answer to education? What could a country where Black people are murdered in broad daylight by police at a rate over twice that of white people possibly know anything about a peaceful society? What could the country where police murder more of its citizens total than any other developed nation possibly know about innocent until proven guilty? What could a country with over 800 *official* military bases worldwide (all conveniently placed near rich deposits of natural resources) possibly know about liberty? What could a country that makes lobbying senators and congressmen legal possibly know about democracy? What could the country with 6 empty houses to every 1 homeless person know about opportunity? What could a handful of rich, white, slave owning men possibly know about establishing a free, just, and equal society?

We're told that the freedom of speech and the right to vote constitute two of the most important benchmarks for a free, democratic, and just society. An examination of how these ideals are practiced in the U.S. shows that freedom, equality and justice are only reserved for a select few.

What good is having the right to speak when the people we're speaking to have no reason to care about what we have to say. When what we have to say doesn't gather power fast enough to fight against their money, it demonstrates that their money speaks louder than our words. And they know that. So, we're afforded the right to free speech because all they have to do is use their money to maintain the status quo and still offer the illusion that Amerika is a free country without actually being one. While we're spinning our wheels speaking as loud as we can and thanking God that we live in a country where we're not persecuted for doing so, the people with the power - both political and capital - sit back and watch as our speeches, marches, and rallies continuously fall short of the power necessary for real, substantial change. All they have to do is either use their money to counteract the potential for progressive change or back-door any legislation that may threaten the current state of affairs at which point the status quo of unequal power and wealth distribution stays in place. They don't have to persecute us for our speech when they know that they have the power to block any change our speech may otherwise make. Which in itself is a form of persecution. If they can prevent our speech from making any real significant changes, do we really have freedom of speech?

What good is having the right to vote when all the candidates have to conform to the system they're being elected to in order to get any cooperation from it? If we take a closer look at the role our elected officials play in our political system, we see that, no matter who we vote for, it can never count as a guarantee for democracy, freedom, and equality. As such, neither can participation in the political system qualify anyone as being free and equal. Time and time again politicians are elected to office based on promises and policies that they continually fail to uphold. They fail to uphold them because these promises and policies contradict the way the system functions. It's not necessarily that they don't intend to keep these promises and uphold these policies when they initially voice them. It's that once they get into office, they find that the system is much bigger and stronger than they themselves are. No one can join an organization without becoming a part of it. Amerika's political organization is no different. Furthermore, never has a candidate represented Black people's interests as a whole. And what would happen if a viable candidate actually did come out in full representation of the Black community? As was previously mentioned, the Black community only makes up 14% of the population. So even if every single Black person who is eligible voted for this candidate, it still would not be enough to elect this candidate to office. As also previously mentioned, on the off chance that a candidate who truly represented the interests of Black, poor and working-class people managed to actually get elected, the representation that this candidate would bring to the political stage would immediately be stifled and compromised by the much larger and much more powerful white supremacist Amerikan political machine which is driven by money. It makes no difference who is in office if the rules and customs that have to be followed are dictated by interests that contradict those of the person in office and the people who put them there. Eventually, this representative who initially had the people's interests at heart would have to conform to the way the political system operates in order to get any cooperation. Ultimately, it's not the people who elected the official that the representative has to answer to. It's the people with more immediate power and money that control the elected official. This is along the same lines of the point that the Black Panthers proved in 1968 when they ran Eldridge Cleaver for president.

Similarly, modern candidates continuously get elected on the idea of restoring the middle class along with its pride and dignity. What often goes overlooked is that in order for there to be a middle, there also has to be an upper and a lower. Any candidate that wants to "restore the middle class" is implying that they're ok with having a lower class. In other words, this candidate is okay with the existence of poverty. And who in this country - in this world - as a whole, has been kept in a state of perpetual poverty?

This is the system that Black people were integrated into. Once they were integrated into it, they were placed at the bottom of it. Because while segregation may have been officially outlawed, racism was not. And as the most durable and dynamic social construct ever created, racism inevitably found other ways to enforce itself.

White society wasn't, and isn't, the pinnacle of freedom and democracy. But when Black people are forced to spend day in and day out being face to face with treatment by white people that was worse than how white people were themselves being treated, the desire to be included in that society becomes immediate and intense enough to overshadow a more critical analysis of white society. The focus became more intensified on the elimination of the "separate" part to the point that the "equal" part was overlooked. This is why Malcolm X was able to see what Martin Luther King still yet could not, but eventually did.

What does not get taught to us in schools is that being separated from white society is not what made segregation in the Jim Crow south bad for Black people. Segregation was bad for Black people because even though they were separated from white people and white society, white people and white society still had control over their lives. It's not like they were free to make their own laws, create their own education system and curriculum, hold their own elections, or decide how their politicians were allowed to operate in their respective roles. They were not left to determine their own economic system, have their own constitution, practice their own health care, or even create their own justice system. All of this was still being determined and enforced by white people.

White society wasn't, and isn't, the pinnacle of freedom and democracy. But when Black people are forced to spend day in and day out being face to face with treatment by white people that was worse than how white people were themselves being treated, the desire to be included in that society becomes immediate and intense enough to overshadow a more critical analysis of white society. This is what Malcolm X understood that Martin Luther King still yet could not, but finally did.

When we idealize the functions of Amerikan society, it is an automatic assumption that everyone who participates within that society is in the most ideal possible situation they can be. Whether it be an unintentional oversight or a malicious attempt at keeping Black people where we think they belong, this idealization of Amerikan society amounts to implicit racism on our part.

So now it's time to ask ourselves, do we still agree with Rev. Dr. Martin Luther King, Jr.? If not, are we prepared to be public about our disagreement with him? More importantly, are we prepared to face the inevitable social assumption and very accurate implication that our newfound disagreement with him makes us racist?

Chapter 4
Cultural Appropriation

Culture is imperative for the human spirit to thrive. Culture is necessary for humans to feel connected with a sense of purpose, individuality, and knowledge of self. Any society that lacks culture will inevitably breed a population with an identity crisis. This identity crisis stems from a combination of two things. One, the lack of security in who they are as individuals and two, wanting to be dissociated from the pathologies, malfeasance, and repugnant aspects that accompany a society without culture i.e. racism, classism, sexism. In an attempt to reconcile the conflict and satisfy the feeling of dissociation, the craving for culture tends to compel the human spirit to gravitate towards the strongest and most prevalent culture that it comes into contact with. Factions from a society without culture will inevitably attempt to adopt certain facets and characteristics of the culture closest and most influential to it. In the case of white Amerika that happens to be Black culture. Certain expressions of culture from growing dread locks and adopting unnatural speech patterns to emulating the music and using the nomenclature are all manifestations of the misguided attempt to shed the racist based identity that we as white people are born into. This is called cultural appropriation.

Cultural appropriation is essentially the theft of another culture. Cultural appropriation occurs when a member of a dominant culture, takes on aspects of another culture that has been oppressed by that dominant group. The historical intent behind cultural appropriation varies. However, the effects have always been the same. The person who culturally appropriates is usually awarded benefits and notoriety such as admiration, money, and even credit for starting a trend. However, the original culture that was appropriated gets mistreated and vilified for doing the exact same thing. For instance, cornrows were considered "ghetto" in a derogatory sense until white girls started wearing them. Then they were a hot new fad. Listening to rap music was associated with criminals until suburban kids decided to start listening to it. Then every white kid with mediocre rhymes was chasing a music career. Cultural appropriation results in the weakening of said culture's direct relationship with the people to whom it belongs. Thus, this weakening of the relationship dilutes the culture's effects in solidifying the identity of those people.

Cultural appropriation carries with it some of the more cryptic ways racism manifests. When we appropriate another culture, we influence society's association of that culture with people from whom it does not originate. It is a form of identity nullification. Since culture is a fundamental necessity for building and securing identity, distorting a culture as well as its association with a certain people, effectively strips the people from which the culture originated of their own identity. Stripping people of their culture and identity is an exact tactic that was used to subjugate Black people during chattel slavery. During chattel slavery, Black people were robbed of their names, their language, their religion, their land, their customs, their traditions, their music and everything else that goes into forming a complete culture. Taking away a people's culture takes away a people's identity. And taking away a people's identity cripples their will and determination for freedom. By taking away the identity of a people, they are dehumanized. This dehumanization leaves them susceptible for a new identity to be placed on them. This new identity is one that is forced upon them by the slave owner who instills a new identity based upon the dependence of and submission to the slave owner.

After chattel slavery came the Jim Crow south during which the culture of Black and Native people was portrayed as inferior, dirty, low class, evil, and immoral. While forced to live day – to – day life facing deprecation, humiliation and ever-present threat of violence, Black and Native people were also subjected to the demonization of their culture. Jazz musicians were widely considered by white people to be criminals and junkies. The religions of Hoodoo, Voodoo, Vodou, and Santeria were then, and still now, considered to be satanic, evil, and dangerous. The English vernacular used by Black people, particularly in the south, was held to be lowbrow and ignorant. Black culture was consistently made the target of white humor and entertainment. From black face and watermelon to Mammy and the angry Black woman, stereotypes about Black people and Black culture were continuously degraded as a source for white amusement. Even in the north, Black and Native people were expected to conform to white society and, in fact, had to do so just to survive. While segregation may not have been law, racist attitudes still permeated every basic function of society. Black and Native people were still expected to at least socially submit to white people and were often chastised and humiliated for equating themselves with us.

Cultural appropriation can also combine other unintentional expressions of racism with itself to form a whole new expression of it. Combining fetishism with cultural appropriation often leads white people to believe that we now have access into the community we fetishize because we've adopted their culture and have friends, partners, or even kids that are of another race and culture. These relationships cause us to believe that we can now be a part of this community. The added attitude of feeling entitled to access the Black community by proxy is indicative of an identity crisis. This identity crisis arises from a desire to not be racist which conflicts with an identity that was created by racism. This conflict is manifested as the overcompensation of trying to prove to the world that we're not racist. These overcompensating efforts result in the appropriation of culture.

By attempting to assume the aspects or characteristics of an oppressed community and trying to insert ourselves into that community, we are just displaying another form of racism. There's absolutely nothing wrong with trying to shed the whiteness we've been indoctrinated with. This is, in fact, a necessary step towards eradicating racism. But appropriating the culture and identity of another race to do so only perpetuates the whiteness we're trying so desperately to rid ourselves of.

White identity in the modern form is built on racism. Without subjugating and dominating others, we would have no idea who we are. This is because modern day culture for white people was established by racism. With the advent of capitalism and the idea to use race-based chattel slavery as the means to build it, white Europeans decided that they wanted all of the money but didn't want to do any of the work. Thus, the most brutal, dehumanizing, violent, and rapacious form of slavery the world has ever seen is developed and instituted. Obscene amounts of wealth and fortune are built by the people who would never see one dime of it; who, in fact, paid for it with their own lives. Fast forward to today, and the society we live in is the same one that was built on the backs of people who were subject to this egregious slavery simply because their skin was a different color than ours.

The institution of capitalism and the rise of chattel slavery effectively separated white people from our own cultural heritage. Before the spread of Christianity and capitalism, white European culture was as rich and sacred as anywhere else in the world. But with the dawn of capitalism paid for by slavery, white Europeans and all those descended from European countries are effectively left without an authentic and organic culture. Without culture, the only thing left to build an identity on is the only way that we are able to relate to the rest of the world.

For centuries, white people have vilified and degraded the culture, appearance, characteristics, language, and social norms of Black, Brown and indigenous people as being "inferior", "barbaric", "savage" or "uncivilized". When combined with the unimaginable trauma of being kidnapped from your family, stuffed like cargo on a boat for months, taken overseas to a foreign land completely unfamiliar, subjected to the most vile, vicious, despicable forms of violence, and forced to do back-breaking labor 13, 15, 18 hours a day in the sweltering heat, identity is one of the only things that can keep a person's sanity. But Black people were robbed of that too. When your land is invaded by foreign people who spit in the face of your hospitality, try to enslave you, then intentionally mass murder 75% of your people through disease, war, and famine only to repeatedly violate peace treaties, fail to deliver agreed upon food and supplies as compensation for land as well as out right displace the few remaining survivors in order to rape your land for natural resources, all while flooding what little society you have left with drugs and alcohol, identity is the one thing that can keep you connected with your roots. But Native people were forced to watch as theirs was effectively obliterated right before their eyes.

Although none more acutely felt than Black and Native, in one way or another, people of any other race or culture outside of the white Eurocentric Amerikan standard have faced the annihilation of their identity through the arrogance of white people shamelessly trying to separate people from their culture and replace it with ours all while capitalizing on theirs as we make it our own. As it stands, it is imperative for Black, Native, Brown, and Asian people to hold on to their culture as tightly as possible. In particular, Black people in Amerika and Europe need every bit of their own culture due to the desecration and loss of it they endured through chattel slavery. Chattel slavery removed Black people from every form of their culture to the point that they have no or very little connection to their own land and heritage. Despite being of the oldest cultures in the world, they have literally been forced to rebuild their culture from the ground up according to circumstances that were beyond their control.

It should be noted that cultural appropriation is different from cultural appreciation, cultural exchange, and cultural assimilation. Cultural appreciation is when a member from a dominant, oppressive culture recognizes the validity, sanctity, and beauty of another culture and pays due homage to it. Cultural exchange is when members from one culture actively invite members from another culture to take part in theirs. Cultural assimilation is when members from an oppressed culture are forced to assimilate to oppressive culture in order to survive. Nevertheless, for us to come along and try to take culture away from people who are already oppressed and not only make it our own while vilifying them for it but, also profiting from it, be it intentionally malicious or not, is racist.

Chapter 5
The White Hero Complex

There are some of us who don't see how even seemingly the most charitable and benevolent acts of compassion can be racist. Some of us put so much effort into helping the world and trying to make it a better place that we become completely oblivious to how our actions are doing just the opposite. What's worse is that we miss the "why". We don't understand why missionary trips to Africa, using flies on the lips of Black children to tug at heartstrings and pocketbooks, and inserting our opinions into conversations about how to deal with, survive, and eliminate racism are counterproductive and racist. We want so badly to help the world and to solve the problems that our narrow focus prevents us from seeing the bigger picture.

So, what is the bigger picture? It's called the white savior complex, the white hero complex, or some variation thereof. The white savior complex is a thought process in which we ultimately end up placing our own selfish interests and egos ahead of the real issue. In most cases we actually use the real issue as a means for satisfying our own self-interests and egos. We place more importance on the role we play or the benefits we gain from our involvement rather than effecting change in a way that doesn't perpetuate the very issue we're fighting against.

The philanthropic endeavors of the Christian Children's Fund, Catholic Charities, and the Bill and Malinda Gates Foundation are perfect examples of how white people use Black suffering to make themselves appear divine, satisfy our delusions of grandeur, and in the process, funnel money into our own pockets. This appearance, however, has consequences that sometimes go overlooked. The first is to appease the ego. By putting effort into supposed acts of charity, we are able to feel better about ourselves. We are now able to sleep soundly while under the impression that we've helped people who need it. By helping people who need it we start to gain an undeserved sense of superiority. By choosing compassion towards the downtrodden, we begin to feel as though we are owed something by them. At which point our compassion turns to entitlement. Entitlement turns to superiority when we feel that we have leverage over anyone, including those we've helped, who would have the audacity to call our character into question. We focus less on the methods we use to improve society and more on the way it makes us feel to do so. The second consequence philanthropy produces is to disempower the people who are oppressed. By nature, oppression is disempowering. It keeps the people who are affected by it from being self-determined. They are robbed of the power to determine their own destiny. By disempowering the people who are oppressed, charities are able to create a dependence. The people who are suffering are now dependent on the charity for their reprieve. This dependence is not only self-perpetuating but, it also opens the door for exploitation. Nonprofit organizations are built on this premise. Massive amounts of money are made using the people who are suffering as the pretext for donations and funding. Yet very little of that money goes towards the people whose suffering was used as a social guilt trip to amass it.

In 2010, when an earthquake devastated Haiti leaving tens of thousands of people homeless, hungry, and stranded, the Red Cross stepped in to help. Promising to rebuild homes, roads, schools, and more, the Red Cross got to work on raising funds, asking for people to donate whatever they could. It was one of their most successful campaigns to date, raising nearly half a billion dollars. Five years later, they had built a grand total of six houses for permanent residence. Six. Ten years later, that money is still unaccounted for.

In the early months of 2020, news broke from Mississippi's state auditor who announced that at least $4 million in federal welfare money was stolen by John Davis, the head of the state welfare agency who conspired with Nancy New, the director of the Mississippi Community Education Center and New Learning Resources. Money that was supposed to go to help people in poverty was being embezzled by a powerful government official. The Mississippi Community Education Center, which operates as Families First for Mississippi, is a nonprofit agency that provides programs like youth development, parenting education, workforce readiness, literacy promotion, addiction education and obesity education, all of which were supposed to be funded by the $4 million embezzled by the director. You may be asking yourself how this could be related to racism. How embezzling money from a random nonprofit racist? It just so happens that Mississippi is not only the poorest state in the U.S. but, is also over 37% Black. Contrasted to the entire United States, which is made up of only 14% Black people, it would seem that the majority of the families that suffer from poverty in Mississippi are Black.

In addition to this money, the very destructive mentality of the savior that gets inflated with every act of benevolence, becomes normalized in society and as such, fades into the background so that it exists at a very subconscious level - both individually as well as socially. On the edge of downtown Minneapolis is the Sharing and Caring Hands compound and Mary's Place, founded by Mary Jo Copeland in 1985. From the outside, The Sharing and Caring Hands building looks much like a sports arena. The front door is equipped with an amusement-park-ride style waiting line to accommodate the hordes of poor people that depend on her for help. This line leads into a cafeteria style facility where she provides over 3000 hot meals a week. On the Sharing and Caring Hands website, it says there are over 3,300 beds for people who would otherwise have no place comfortable to sleep. They provide personal hygiene facilities, dental care, and every year give out clothes to thousands of people from their clothing closet as well as around 500,000 lbs of food. Sharing and Caring Hands also provides 100 fully furnished transitional apartments for homeless families with children which can house over 600 people, 400 of whom are kids known as Mary's Place. In addition to all of this, Sharing and Caring hands provides bus passes, money for cell phone bills, and eye exams, all of which is funded with private money. Mary Jo Copeland is very proud of the fact that she takes no public money from the government. She is 100% donation financed, only 9% of which, goes towards staffing and overhead. The other 91% is goes to providing for people in need. In light of all that Mary Jo does for poor people, one would think she's the closest thing to Mother Teresa the U.S. has. However, there's a very important perspective that seems to be missing from the narrative that surrounds

Mary Jo and her charity. To begin with, I personally have been to Mary Jo's to ask for help. The process that one has to go through is one that is especially humiliating. We are required to stand in line just like any other place. Hence, the reason for the amusement-park-ride style ramp leading up to the front door. This line then goes up a short flight of stairs and in through the double doors of the cafeteria. Once inside the cafeteria, the line stretches all the way to the back of the room where the food is being served through windows in front of which stands Mary Jo herself. To get assistance for Sharing and Caring Hands, one is required to wait in this line until it is their turn to ask Mary Jo personally. At this point, Mary Jo will ask a series of questions as they pertain to one's specific situation. After these questions are answered, Mary Jo will give her decision on whether or not she will help. All of this is done in front of an entire cafeteria full of people. Those who come to her for help are literally made to grovel at her feet in front of an entire room full people watching. Additionally, there doesn't seem to be any mention of these people getting connected with social workers through Sharing and Caring Hands. Why? Moreover, are the people who are getting paid to work at Sharing and Caring Hands also people that have come to her for help? It seems that Mary Jo could be taking the time to educate these people on the causes of their circumstances and organizing them into an empowered, self-sustaining community. This is, of course, assuming that she herself understands the root causes of poverty. If Mary Jo does understand the root causes of poverty, it means that she is deliberately keeping these people uninformed. One can only assume the reasons why she would do this however, based on what we already know about the white hero complex, it's quite possible, and even probable, that Mary Jo's white hero complex preys on the ignorance of the impoverished in order to keep them dependent on her. On the other hand, if Mary Jo does not understand the root causes of poverty, it simply means that she believes poverty to be the fault of those who experience it. In this case, Mary Jo is a victim blamer and as such, her white hero complex preys on the shame of the impoverished people that come to her for help. Either way, it seems clear that Mary Jo's charity has more to do with satisfying her personal interests than it does with empowering poor people and eliminating poverty. In light of this new perspective, it should come as no surprise that in every picture on the Sharing and Caring Hands website of Mary Jo, she is accompanied by a child of color. Nonetheless, it remains that if you've built both an entire city block, as well as a local reputation dedicated to "helping" poor people only to find yourself waking up 35 years later doing the exact same thing, then you have not, in fact, helped poor people. You've kept them dependent on you in order to feed your white savior complex. If you were actually helping poor people, the number of people coming to you for help would decrease, not increase. If you have the means, you can either help to empower poor people become self-determined as a community, or you can keep them dependent on you for their livelihood. One of these options puts the altruistic interest of poor people first. The other puts the self-centered interest of the ego first. Evidently, The Red Cross, former head of the Mississippi welfare agency John Davis and his co-conspirator Nancy New, were more than happy to appear as though they were helping poor Black people, all the while, lining their pockets with money that was supposed to be spent doing just that. While Mary Jo Copeland evidently cares less for the money than she does for the glory.

The irony in white heroism and philanthropic racism is the failure to see how the programs and charities that are supposedly set up to help these people, do absolutely nothing to attack or alter the system that keeps Black, Brown, and Native people in a perpetual cycle of oppression. The most overlooked racist issue with engaging in philanthropy and charity work is that it functions on assumption rather than analysis. Philanthropy under capitalism either fails or refuses to analyze the political, economic, and social systems of our society that poverty and racism are symptoms of. Instead, it operates under the assumption that our society is as good as it will ever get, and that poverty and racism are inevitable circumstances that charity can triage while we deal with it. But that they will never be fully eradicated.

Furthermore, charity and philanthropy deal with poverty by placing the responsibility on the victim. Things like financial literacy courses and job-readiness seminars insinuate that people living in poverty would be able to get out if only they would stop spending money on weekly lattes and made themselves more exploitable for the labor force when the real cause is the refusal to pay livable wages and the actual availability of jobs. It is the epitome of the western, Euro-Amerikan way of life to treat the symptoms rather than cure the cause. But if white people can use the treatment of these symptoms to make ourselves look and feel like Gods, then we will deny the cause and hide the cure with everything we've got.

Nevertheless, often times, even at a subconscious level, we become motivated to join the fight for a particular cause that may appeal to us in order to make life and society better for the future. For whatever reason, we make the conscious decision to take action in hopes to progress the movement and make some semblance of improvement. However, as white people, we often do so with very destructive presumptions. As mentioned in the previous chapter, most of us will take a very arrogant approach when joining these causes. We often think that we have the perfect solutions, and as such that we are the de facto authority on the matter. Any attempts to disagree, redirect the conversation, or even offers to help us broaden our understanding of our place in the movement are met with defensiveness, hostility and derision. This comes from a pre-conditioned mentality at a very deep seated, subconscious level that Black, Brown, and Native people are inherently dumber, weaker, and more incompetent than us. We hold a core belief that was ingrained in us since birth that if left to their own devices, oppressed people would never be able to facilitate their own freedom. This core belief offers us the opportunity to swoop in and play the messianic role of savior. Now our egos have found a plentiful supply of stroking and feeding. Our motivation for participating in the movement becomes one that places the importance of our own self-centered satisfaction and egotistical gratification above progressing the struggle and helping the cause.

In the end, there are those of us who really do want to help. In fact, most of us do. However, our reasons for doing so are misguided. By feeling sorry for oppressed people, we ultimately feel as though they're helpless and, subsequently, weaker than ourselves. However, these feelings exist in a subconscious framework that we're mostly unaware of. Due to our misunderstanding of racism, many of us attempt to enter the fight against racism with very good intentions. However, the results are a much more accurate reflection of our true beliefs, even if we ourselves do not see it. This is why we have to be critical enough of the actions that our intentions drive us to and humble enough to accept the critique we may receive.

Chapter 6
Tokenism

There is no doubt that representation is important. People who have traditionally faced oppression have also had that oppression exacerbated through the constant prevention to be connected with the esteem of public positions and the widespread respect that accompanies greatness when witnessed by the public eye. When people who have had their humanity systematically stripped from them continually come face to face with unrelatable content in everyday life, being able to see themselves in positions of high regard becomes a valuable step in reaffirming their humanity. Little Black, Brown, and Native boys and girls need to be able to see that they can achieve more than what the rest of society is telling them. They need to know that even under a white supremacist system, their fates are not sealed simply because they are not white. They need to know that even though the entire deck is stacked against them, they are still just as capable and valuable as little white boys and girls. By seeing positive images of people who look like themselves in the public eye, oppressed people can combat the message of alienation that society has consistently delivered to them, abandon the mind state of self-hatred and deprecation that accompanies the aforementioned message, as well as begin to repair and heal from the damage that message does to the human psyche. Nevertheless, with all of that said, it is incumbent upon us to realize that not all representation is good representation. When we hear marginalized and disenfranchised peoples talk about the importance of representation, most white people get a very distorted idea of what significance that has to Black and other oppressed people. We have a propensity to perceive these representations as indicative of "progress" or even evidence against charges of racism. This is because most people who are racist, have no idea that they are racist. And they have no idea that they're racist because the average white Amerikan or European does not understand racism. The typical white person understands racism in a very limited scope.

Most white people will have one, two, or even a handful of Black friends. We'll see images of Black and Brown people right alongside white people in movies and television. We see Black people hold political offices and promoted to corporate positions of power. And when we see all this, we think that it's a sign that racism is ending. However, due to such a limited understanding of racism, most white people believe that their Black friend automatically absolves them of racism. By including a Black person in our leisurely photos on social media, we tend to have a very distorted view of how we think the world sees us. We believe that Black people playing roles in movies and on tv that are adjacent to white roles that it's indicative of the benefits of integration. We think that Black people in political offices and board rooms means society has done away with the ugliness and grotesque nature of racism as we understand it. We think that these displays of inclusion are symptomatic of being enlightened and progressive. We assume an internalized feeling of superiority to the racists of the Jim Crow south and portray an attitude that spending amicable time with a Black person means that we're unable to be racist. This type of racism is called tokenism. Tokenism is a very lazy, uninterested, or merely symbolic effort at representation or inclusion of Black people within society. It's a way to give the appearance of equality without actually allowing Black people to have the power that's necessary for social equality to exist.

With this understanding, however, we can see that the role of token is one that is decidedly powerless. More often than not, if a Black person is with a white dominant group of friends, the white cultural experience will not only prevail, but will also expect the Black friend to conform to the norms and values of the white cultural experience in order maintain inclusivity and acceptance. Neither is it likely that this white dominant group of friends to have the presence of mind to learn about the Black person's culture, struggles, and experiences. Virtually never would any of the white friends even consider that their Black friend's culture and experience in the world is any different from their own. Nor would any of them have the wherewithal to try and gain some appreciation for Black culture. At least not without appropriating it.

When we consider movies and television programs that are dominantly white cast, we can, with almost perfect certainty, predict the role of the Black person. This is because those roles are specifically fit to fulfill a stereotype.

Horror movie: Black person gets killed early so as to introduce the movie's antagonist character. Teen comedy: dark skin Black Male plays supporting role as a superlative school athlete and/or goofy comedic relief from dramatic scenes with quippy one liners. Dark skin female plays supporting role as lead role's best friend with either overly promiscuous or overly aggressive and intimidating attitude both of which are usually used in comedic context to elicit humor. Light skin Black Male plays one dimensional aesthetically superlative school heartthrob with little to no substance. Light skin female often plays similar role. Both often depicted as mysterious and untouchable with very little character development and insight into the depths of those roles. Romantic comedy: not much different than teen comedy. Thriller: black person, often Male, cast in a supporting role as either the strong and intimidating secondary character or as the villain itself with any of the characteristics that portray the villainous role. Drama: black person cast as the wise and sagacious best friend whose sole purpose in the movie is to help guide the protagonist through whatever tumultuous predicament the writers have come up with. I think you get the point.

In political office and board rooms, the situations are both very similar to each other. The token is expected to play the role of lackey; a yes man/woman. They are expected to spend day in and day out yasuhbossing and be grateful for the opportunity to do so. Under threat of losing their position, cooperation, or support, speaking out about anything that may contradict the interests of white supremacist capitalist business models presents a very real threat. Cast as the token, a Black person, or any other person of color, particularly women, is expected to surrender any and all individual thoughts and opinions. While there is no doubt that the people who arise to these esteemed positions deserve to be there, they face the stifling and degrading experience of being pigeonholed into their role as "seen and not heard." Their merit alone was undoubtedly fought harder for than their white counterparts and referenced as the basis for being placed in these positions. However, now that they are in these positions of high regard, it is specifically their merits, acumen, shrewdness, and least of all, intelligence, that their colleagues are interested in. The tokenism that Black and other people of color in these positions are subjected to is a mechanism that serves to suppress any semblance of their own ideas.

The world of both politics and business are dirty, duplicitous, underhanded, crooked, and highly competitive. As such, Black people and people of color have to compete at an exponentially higher level just to achieve the same positions and benefits as their white competition only to find out that once they actually beat out their white competition, they still face the condescension, patronizing atmosphere, and underestimation that the white people they were competing against never would have to. Essentially, what it means is that Black people and people of color have sacrificed more and therefore, have more to lose by stepping out of or challenging the token role they're cast into.

Furthermore, tokenism has the added effect of placing dual burdens on the shoulders of those assigned to the role of token. The responsibility of validation as well as spokesperson will ultimately rest on the one or two Black people within any white dominated group. More often than not, the weight of these burdens are assumed without the token's consent or awareness. Acting as though Black people are monolithic and that one Black person can easily be substituted for another is the underlying presumption within the tokenist practice.

As spokesperson, the tokenized Black person or person of color is expected to represent the entire Black community as a whole. On questions of Black culture, Black beliefs, Black news, Black perspective, or Black controversy, the tokenized Black person is the assumed expert and as such, is thought to speak for the Black community as a whole. In essence, the tokenized Black or other person of color is a conduit condition which white people can fulfill their desire for Black voyeurism. This assumption extends to the entirety of the Black, Brown, or Native community respectively and whatever the perspective or opinion of the token is, the rest of the white dominated group then assumes that all Black people's opinions and perspectives must be the same.

Similarly, as the validator, any Black person or other person of color belonging to a specific white dominated group is considered an automatic validation of the actions, practices, standards, and beliefs of said group. As such, the group claims to be inclusive, equal, and ethical simply by the presence and participation of a minority within the group. This validation occurs regardless of how they may feel personally about the standards and practices of the group. Mostly, because the token is often left out of any conversation that challenges the group's dynamics and is simply used as a tool for evidence. "I'm not racist. I have a Black friend." "We're not racist. We have Black people on the board of directors." "I'm not racist, my girlfriend/boyfriend is Black", "Amerikkka isn't racist. We had a Black president". Weaponizing Black people in an attempt to disprove your racism is racist. It places them in the position of tokens and disempowers them. It's also patronizing to the entire Black community by assuming that the Black community is gullible enough and ignorant enough to think that the whole of racism can be completely evaporated just by proximity to Black people. Have you ever asked your Black friend how they feel about being the only reason you're not racist?

To some, in fact, to most white people, the racism of tokenism that essentially depends on the idea of diversity is as ironic as it is enigmatic. We don't understand how diversity could possibly be racist because the way we were taught about racism is that segregation and hate were the most recent and severe forms of racism. If segregation based on hate is what racism is, then integration based on love must be the opposite of racism, right? Wrong. Just because Black people are included in it doesn't mean they had a hand in creating it. It doesn't mean they had a say in how it functions. Black people's inclusion in the social, economic, or political functions and institutions of society does not mean they are included in the decisions made therein, nor does it mean they have a hand in which direction those functions, and institutions take within our society. And this is tokenism. When white people bring one or two Black people along for the ride to give the appearance of diversity and a progressive, non-racist culture yet systematically bar them from any real power to affect their own lives.

Yes, representation matters. But only as far as it helps to restore a sense of self-worth and identity. The minute white people start using the idea of Black representation to push our own agendas forward, it stops being representation. Trying to hinge Black people's sense of self-worth and identity on what we consider to be success is when it starts being tokenism. Thinking that we set the bar for greatness is supremacist ideology. White people do not set the bar for greatness. Black excellence is not defined by what we consider to be successful. Tokenism is when Black people are included in society but not involved in society.

Chapter 7
Color Blind Racism

White people have two distinct mind sets that influence our approach to colorblindness. Both of them are rooted in attempts to reject racism. However, they also both proceed from a drastic misunderstanding of racism. One of them is a mindset that attempts to place love at the forefront of our personal attempts to not be racist. It's a good first step headed in the wrong direction. The other is a mindset of pity combined with uncomfortability. Hoping racism won't rear its ugly head by pretending race doesn't exist because talking about it makes you more uncomfortable than it makes Black people is not even a good first step. Both of these mind sets present themselves as attempts to not be racist by refusing to acknowledge race. Ironically, this is also what makes them racist.

The first mindset is one that exhibits a thinly veiled attempt to pretend that one does not in fact even notice skin color. It is then further exacerbated by white people who confuse prejudice with racism. A lot of society as a whole have a tendency to believe that prejudice based on skin color is the same as racism. As previously discussed in earlier chapters, while one involves the other, they are, in fact, not interchangeable. Nevertheless, while it is categorically incorrect, it is from this misunderstanding that the first mind set of colorblind racism stems.

This mindset is grossly misinformed by the saying that goes "love sees no color". This adage attempts to create an image in our minds of what the ideal society free from racism might look like. Of course, it would be ideal to live in a society where the color of one's skin and one's culture were not the basis for an unequal distribution of power. And although that isn't the world we live in, that is the world that this saying would one day like to apply to. Therefore, this saying states itself as a goal. The idea that "love sees no color" is an end. It's a place we would like to get to as a society. But it is not a tactic for reaching that goal. Using "love sees no color" is not a way for us to get to that place. Not seeing color will not undo racism. Unfortunately, many of the white people who subscribe to this ideology have tried to use it as a tactic for reaching a state in their personal lives where those circumstances are a reality. But to do so is both a false statement considering the obvious nature of color and cultural differences as well as further upholding racism by a refusal to recognize essential parts of Black people's identity, be it intentional or not.

To make matters worse, the attitude that often accompanies the first mind set of colorblind racists is one that tries to deny any further responsibility of eliminating racism from society beyond that of personal beliefs and practices. It's the very selfish, arrogant, and sectarian notion that eliminating racist attitudes and beliefs - no matter how misguided those efforts might be - from our own lives is enough to make us good people and that the rest of racism in society isn't our problem. So, while our desire to eliminate racism is admirable, its lacking in thorough analysis and is rooted in a very selfish perspective of racism. It doesn't come from an interest in the complete annihilation of racism from society but, only an interest in one's own personal projection of it.

A lot of us have tried to use the colorblind method as a way to reach a society free of racism. To say that love sees no color is to envision a society where all people are loved equally among each other regardless of color and culture. As Martin Luther King, Jr said, "...where they are judged not by the color of their skin, but the content of their character. " This quote by Dr. Martin Luther King, Jr serves as a reinforcement for colorblind racist white people's justification for rejecting the presence of a difference in skin color and culture.

The saying intends to promote the ideology that we should live and respect all skin colors equally. Unfortunately, due to white people's gross misunderstanding of racism however, quite a few of us have a tendency to take this maxim and completely twist its meaning into something that suits our comfort level with racism rather than rid ourselves of it. We misinterpret what it means and apply it incorrectly to our attempts at not being racist. The idea that racism requires hate causes us to believe that if we practice what we believe to be the opposite of hate then it will make us the opposite of racist. Since most of us understand love to be the opposite of hate, we naturally conclude that if we fail to recognize skin color then it means we love our fellow human and therefore have achieved full non-racist status. We then take this one step further and start to believe that if everyone else did this as well, then we could achieve a racist-free society. However, the saying that "love sees no color" as well as the quote by Dr. King, do not state that we should not acknowledge skin color and culture. They merely define themselves as an invalid basis for love and judgment. Nevertheless, as we've previously discussed, hate is not a requirement for racism. Therefore, if we understand love to be the opposite of hate, then it cannot be a requirement for non-racism.

Moreover, in order to be used as reinforcement, the quote by Dr. King has been taken out of context. White people have this very distorted misconception that his words apply to us the same way they apply to the Black people he was speaking about. They do not. In order for Dr. Martin Luther King, Jr's words from his "I Have a Dream" speech to apply equally to white people the same way they apply to Black people, there would first have to be an equal disbursement of social, economic, and political power among white and Black people. Since the evidence that proves there is not an equal disbursement of power is overwhelming, and since Dr. King was speaking about racism, his words cannot possibly apply to us the same way they do for Black people. For that to happen, we would have to have endured 500 years of chattel slavery, face the reality that no time soon will we be financially compensated for 500 years of our forced free labor, suffered through the prospect of getting lynched just for looking at a white person wrong with no recourse or possibility of justice, face the very likely possibility of getting murdered by police with impunity simply for being Black, struggle with mass incarceration, watch as the U.S. government sponsors the flooding of our neighborhoods with the deadliest and most addicting drugs known to man, then watch as the war on drugs specifically targets and criminalizes us, systemic poverty, and countless other societal issues that plague the Black community all of which were initiated and maintained by white people. The concept of "love sees no color" and being "... judged not by the color of our skin but on the content of our character" would be a Utopian society, there is no doubt. But given the world's history of race relations, it is impossible for us to get there by not acknowledging differences in skin color and culture.

The second mindset that tends to motivate colorblind racism is one that sees a difference in skin color and culture as afflictions. Some of us will refuse to mention it because we think that it's a source of shame or embarrassment or offense if we do. And when we do mention it, we'll say it under our breath for fear that a Black person may hear us, and we'll have to face reproach. Often times, in certain instances, we'll completely omit it from descriptions thinking that declining from using it as an adjective somehow makes us more sensitive and empathetic to the plight of Black people. However, the overlooked and underlying implication in that logic is that we believe that the plight of Black people is being Black instead of an oppressive society being created to oppress them because they are Black.

The failure to recognize skin color is the failure to be non-racist because it is a denial of an essential part of the identity of Black, Brown, Native and all other people of color. Unlike being white, being Black, Brown, Native, and Asian is a source of pride. It has to be simply by reason of racism's attempt to vilify and degrade it. In order to maintain their survival and humanity, Black people have had to fight tooth and nail to assert not only their right to be Black but, to also assert the inherent human equality that Black people have with white people. Black people have had to labor, sweat, bleed, and die to keep their own and each other's sense of self-worth equal to that of white people's. And they've had to do so all in the face of our attempts to undermine that equality. This is why Black pride is not racist. This is why calls for Black power are not racist. Because Black pride and Black power are survival responses. If it weren't for white power and white pride trying to kill and subjugate Black people, there would be no need for Black pride and Black power. However, since we have systematically created the need for Black pride and Black power by denying it and trying to destroy it, the refusal to acknowledge the basis for that pride is racist. Black power is not anti-white. We only think it is because white power is anti-Black. Skin color, culture, and heritage are a crucial part of Black people's identity by sheer virtue of our attempts to strip, rob, degrade, vilify, and demonize it. It is crucial specifically because of our attempts to completely and utterly destroy it in order to subjugate and oppress them.

Although race is a social construct, it is now one that is a very real part of our society. However, as white people, it is imperative we keep in mind that racism doesn't exist because of race. Racism exists because of arrogance, fear, shame, greed, hate, an inferiority complex and, most of all, ignorance. Pretending race doesn't exist won't get rid of racism. Nor will it make you not racist. In fact, quite the opposite on both counts. Even people who are colorblind are able to see in Black and white.

Chapter 8
Cultural Credit

One of the most obscured and overlooked forms of racism is cultural credit and the way we apply it to our society. Cultural credit is the merit that we as a society give to acknowledge the contributions that are made in creating our society's rites, traditions, beliefs, and practices. Everything from music and dance to philosophy and religion, from architecture and invention to hair and clothing styles are essential in the development and continuation of culture. Cultural credit acknowledges and validates all of the different elements that are contributed in order to compose a culture as whole.

However, despite the lack of credit, or even acknowledgment from society, Black people have consistently been the single most dominant contributors to our culture, in both ancient and modern times. Virtually everything we do, say, wear, see, and hear in our modern society has been either a direct result of Black participation or largely influenced by it. Yet not only do we still refuse to acknowledge and credit Black people for their cultural contributions but, we also vilify them for their culture until we decide we want to appropriate it. And, as if that wasn't bad enough, when we do credit Black people for their contributions, we only do when their contributions entertain us. What's even worse is when the acknowledgment itself finally does come, its patronizing and belittling.

We live in a culture glorifies the rich and powerful. Names like Andrew Carnegie and John D. Rockefeller are household names that virtually anybody can recognize. Their names have become synonymous with entrepreneurship, wealth and power. Even more so than the wealthy of modern times like Jeff Bezos, Elon Musk, and Bill Gates due to their longevity and generational industry leading statuses. While Jeff Bezos and Elon Musk may have accumulated more capital, it still tends to pale in comparison by reason of circumstance. When the Rockefellers and Hearsts and the Carnegies began to amass their wealth, it was during a time when Amerika was still in its infancy. The economic and political landscapes were not yet firmly established within the fabric of Amerikan society. As such, they are considered to be the men whose industrialism paved the way for the Bezos and Musks to become what they are.

As categorically and absurdly incorrect as the idea that the founding Amerikan captains of industry amassed their fortune through hard work and perseverance is, glorifying them and their ill-gotten gains is rooted in Amerikan exceptionalism and the false sense of superiority that Amerikan culture has of itself. If it were not for the malicious and intentional exploitation, slavery, and cruel working conditions created by these tyrants, they never would have seen half of the wealth they've become renowned for.

Yet, isn't it interesting, and a little too convenient that we don't hear about how they became so wealthy. Only that they did. It's also interesting that the glorification of wealth and power in Amerika completely and absolutely omits a man by the name of Mansa Musa.

Mansa Musa was the single most wealthy person to ever live. He was worth around $400 billion. That's nearly twice what Jeff Bezos is worth. Still, the majority of Amerikans, or anyone for that matter, have never heard of him. How is it that a culture which places so much value on wealth and power has never heard of the single wealthiest person in human history?

It's the same reason that we've never learned about any other Black wealth owner that wasn't a rapper or ball player. Mansa Musa was a king of Mali at a time when Mali was the world's number one gold supplier. It's because he was wealthy Black man who was a king at a time when the culture of him and his people flourished.

Most conversations fail to include Jay-Z's name in the same breath as Bezos, Musk, or Buffet. Why? It's not that we don't acknowledge Jay-Z's accomplishments. We just don't glorify them the same way we do white wealth owners. We acknowledge Jay's business acumen, but we don't hold it at the same regard we do white men's. And why is that? Why does Amerikan culture have more respect for white wealth than Black wealth? Because even though racism gets its power from capitalism, Black individuals cannot buy their way out of racism. The individual success of a wealthy Black person is no match for the centuries of systemic economic oppression they've had to endure at our hands. Therefore, the culture that surrounds the praise of wealth accumulation was built by white racism. Because it was racism that facilitated the accumulation of wealth. So naturally it will be perpetuated by praising white people who horde wealth.

This is not meant to encourage or support the hoarding of wealth or the greed that motivates it. While white people did not invent the individual accumulation of wealth, we did invent hording it at other people's expense. No, this point was raised merely to illustrate that even when Black people play our games by our rules, their contributions to the culture are still treated as inferior and less valuable than whites'.

The names of Bill Gates and Steve Jobs have basically become synonymous with computers. The two most dominant computer operating systems in the world today have helped to bring technology to levels that at one point, the world could only imagine in sci-fi movies. However, unless you've seen the movie Hidden Figures, which although was a monetary success, faded from the limelight rather quickly, you've probably never heard of Katherine Johnson, Dorothy Vaughan, and Mary Jackson. Before Bill Gates and Steve Jobs had even graduated from college, these three women were instrumental in the space race and it was their genius that allowed John Glenn to be the first person to orbit planet Earth. The technological advances that these three Black women played a vital role in facilitating pushed the ideas of technological capabilities farther than any sci-fi writer had ever thought possible. To glorify the tech genius of Bill Gates and Steve Jobs without first acknowledging the three Black women who opened the door for technological imagination to exist in the first place is to deny the cultural credit due to so many Black women. An interesting side note to this is that the math that computers use to operate today is based on math developed in ancient Ethiopia. Yet, another failure to acknowledge the contributions of Black people.

While Archimedes is widely propagated to be the father of mathematics, it was Thales who introduced math to the Greeks and whose concepts and theories were the foundations for his contemporaries and successors alike, including both Pythagoras and Archimedes. We're taught that the math equations, the way we learn to work through them, the geometrical applications as well as their relations to our material world are all products of these great Greek thinkers, starting with Thales. Thales is the earliest of them all. He lived in pre-Socratic Greece in sixth century B.C.E. That's Greece before the age of Socrates and his philosophical contributions to the world. His contemporary, Pythagoras is renowned in the world of mathematics for his theorem and its usefulness in trigonometry. However, it was from the mind of Thales from which Greek concepts of mathematics first arose. Then Pythagoras, Archimedes, Euclid, and many others followed. What goes untaught however, is Thales's locations of residence. He is known as Thales of Miletus as Miletus, which is an island in the middle of the Aegean Sea that was then part of the Greek empire was his place of birth. However, Thales spent a portion of his life living in a land known by many names, the most common being Kemet on the continent of Africa. The word Kemet literally translates to 'the Black land'. It didn't become known as Egypt until around 100 years after Thales lived there, when it was invaded and occupied by the Macedonians who were another auxiliary Greek state. Nevertheless, it wasn't until after he returned from his stay in Kemet that he began to introduce his knowledge of mathematics, geometry and astronomy to the Greeks. All of these concepts were taught to Thales from the ancient Egyptians who had already long possessed the knowledge that he introduced to the Greek (read: white) world. If it weren't for the ancient Egyptians, and the same knowledge of mathematics, geometry, trigonometry and astronomy that built the oldest pyramids in the world, Thales would never have been able to introduce the numerical concepts we still use to this day. A credit to the civilization of humanity that to this day, still goes unrecognized.

When we think about technology, the vast majority of society tends to picture computers, the internet, cell phones, television and the like. However, that's mostly because the use of modern technology has become so normal in our everyday lives. When we flip on a light switch or get on an elevator, most of us don't even consider the technological advantages that we are utilizing when we do. The technology we use today is often taken for granted by society as a whole. It's safe to assert that most of us don't think about the conveniences that technology has afforded us in our everyday lives. However, to overlook these advantages and conveniences that we take for granted is to discredit the contributions of Black inventors to our society. Particularly considering that not only are we virtually never taught about them but, most of the white European and Amerikan inventors that we're taught about are actually either frauds or thieves. Not to take anything away from the genius of

George Washington Carver. The creativity and intelligence that was necessary to come up with so many uses for a peanut is nothing short of admirable. However, it's important for us to question why he is the only Black inventor that is intentionally taught in the public education system. It would seem that while everything George Washington Carver did with the peanut is fascinating and useful, none of it really served to advance human civilization to the next technological level. When we consider that Black inventors contributed things like the stop light (Garrett Morgan, 1923), the refrigerator (J. Standard, 1891), the stethoscope (Imhotep in ancient Egypt/Kemet), air conditioning (Fredrick Jones, 1949), the elevator, (Alexander Miles, 1867), the fire extinguisher (T.J. Marshall, 1872), the clothes dryer (G.T. Sampson, 1892), and so many others, it becomes clear that Black innovation has virtually set the foundation for the technological age in which we live now. We're told that Thomas Edison invented the light bulb with no mention of the man who worked closely with him and perfected it. The light bulb that Thomas Edison made was expensive, ephemeral, and a fire hazard. It was, in fact, a Black man named Lewis Latimer who invented the carbon filament for the light bulb that made it more affordable, more efficient, and safer.

When it comes to style, the difference in treatment compared with the similarity in look is so obviously different that its palpable. When white people put dreads in their hair, the racist effects reverberate far beyond cultural appropriation. White men with dreads are seen by society as edgy, unique, or a little eccentric. Black men with locks are seen by society as menacing, threatening, or ominous. White men using dread locks to set ourselves apart from the rest of society and express our individuality only adds fuel to the fire of racism because Black men are forced to live under constant scrutiny and judgment just for wearing their hair the same way even though it only grows that way naturally on them. White hair does not naturally lock up. The work we have to put into making our hair look the way it effortlessly grows on Black hair is a testament to its cultural appropriation. And the treatment that white men receive from society for wearing our hair that way is a stark contrast to that of Black people even though, if it weren't for Black people, we wouldn't even have that as a way to style our hair in the first place.

In the case of style, no one on Earth or in history has contributed more style and fashion to culture than Black women. However, no one gets dehumanized and demonized for their style and fashion more than Black women either. Before any trend that has become popular in western culture, it first belonged to Black women.

Once thought by society to be ugly and unattractive, thick lips are now known as "full" and "luscious". For centuries Black women were alienated for theirs. Then Angelina Jolie became popular and all of a sudden, she's celebrated for hers. Now, thick lips have become a widely accepted standard for physical attraction. At one time, a brown complexion was considered to be the basis for inferiority. Now an entire market profits from white women trying to get darker. A curvy figure and a "big booty" were once considered to be synonymous with immorality and an insatiable sexual appetite. Now white women are paying millions per year for breast implants and booty lifts. The Kardashians have become infamous for theirs and it's a basic standard in the porn industry. Whether it's natural or not, white women as a whole have a relatively newfound desire for their bodies and aesthetics to now match what they used to degrade Black women for being born with. This also holds true just the same for hair styles, accessories, and vernacular. Hoop earrings, box braids, cornrows, and modern slang were all once considered "ghetto" and "low class". Phrases such as "hook up", "hit up", "dope", "cool", "whack", and "bling" were all once considered slang that was exclusive to the Black community and thought to be indicative of uneducated and uncivilized people. Now, these words and phrases have become commonplace in society. All of a sudden, idolized white women like Kim Kardashian, Kylie Jenner, or Miley Cyrus are becoming known and praised for their curves, their dancing, or their fashion sense, none of which they ever would have even had if it weren't Black women.

Black people have created and influenced more of our culture with contributions in science, mathematics, agriculture, technology, language, style, music and forms of government than any other group of people in the world. Yet, we are only willing to give them credit when it entertains us. And even then, it's a very patronizing and condescending acknowledgment. The attitudes and beliefs that we once held towards Black face and minstrel shows hasn't changed. It's just taken on a different form of entertainment. We expect ball players to "shut up and dribble". We have proverbial temper tantrums whenever an athlete or actor or musician has the nerve to express an opinion. Let alone one we disagree with. We can't even give credit without being racist. If their endeavors entertain us then we're willing to accept their value and contribution. But only as far as our amusement lasts. And even then, when we do acknowledge their cultural relevance, we approach the acknowledgment with a very smug and superior attitude. Not much different than when a dog does tricks for us. We tell the dog "roll over" or "shake". The dog performs and then when the dog is done, we give him his treat, pat him on the head and tell him what a good boy he is. That's about the same way we approach what little cultural credit we're actually willing to give Black people, despite the fact that if it weren't for Black people, we wouldn't have any culture at all.

Chapter 9
History In Black and White

Ask almost any progressive white person what the biggest problem with Black history month is and they will invariably tell you that it is during the shortest month of the year. Well, I got news for you, this is NOT the biggest problem with Black history month. Although there are a number of problems with Black history month - like the fact that Black history is only officially recognized for a month - the biggest problem with Black history month is the way that Black history is taught. Recognizing Black people during the shortest month of the year was merely a final patronizing concession to Black people's on going fight for equality and liberation. The more sinister aspect of Black history month, and Black history as it is taught by the education system in Amerikkka in general, is that it is taught from a white supremacist perspective. Black history in the education system is used as a tool to keep Black people docile and passive. As such, it is taught in a way that is meant to redeem us for 600 years of chattel slavery (despite what we're taught, race based slavery began at least 200 years earlier when Portugal decided to colonize Africa), nearly 100 years of apartheid, nearly 200 years of being targeted by police, murdered by police, over policed, abused by police, and terrorized by police, 75 years of the prison industrial complex, and countless injustices that have purposely gone unaccounted for. That's one hell of a lot of redemption. No wonder we try to keep Black people under our control. To teach Black history in way that makes us look redeemable from that, it would have to be taught in a way that almost makes us look like... well... Gods. Hey guess what...!? That's exactly the way its taught!

First, what we need to come to terms with, is that Black history did not start with chattel slavery in the Amerikas. Nor did it start with chattel slavery at all. Science has proven beyond a doubt, with empirical evidence that the human race began in Africa. This means that the very first people on earth were Black. It necessarily follows then, that Black people literally have the oldest history in the world. However, the education system, historians, and white supremacist culture have done an excellent job at obscuring and erasing pre-slavery Black history. So, the entire school curriculum begins Black history by teaching both white and Black kids about the so-called "founding fathers" of this country. However, the curriculum completely neglects the fact that the most prominent of them, including George Washington and Thomas Jefferson owned slaves. Sally Hemmings, who was owned, raped, and gave birth as products of that rape by Thomas Jefferson is completely omitted from textbooks. But his drafts of the Declaration of Independence sure aren't. George Washington's treatment of not only the enslaved people he owned but also the Black people under his command in the revolutionary war is enough to make anyone's stomach turn. Despite all the false lessons we're given in school, his teeth were not made of wood. They were real teeth pulled out of the mouths of slaves. The history of this country is so egregious to Black and Native people as well as embarrassing and incriminating to white people that we've literally fabricated some stories and left the facts out of others in order to make ourselves appear more forgivable and manipulate Black and Native people into doing just that.

It's said that those who do not learn from history are doomed to repeat it. It is impossible to learn perceptive and crucial lessons from a history we are never taught. We need to have a white history month. We need to teach the truth about the real nature of our ancestors and the role they played in the development of this country.

We are indoctrinated to believe that Abraham Lincoln played a pivotal role in the relationship between white and Black people in this country. This is false on multiple levels. First, Abraham Lincoln wasn't some mighty champion for human rights and equality. Abraham Lincoln expressly believed in the superiority of white people to Black people. After being accused by Democratic senator Stephen A. Douglas of being a proponent of abolition and equality for Black people during their debates, Abraham Lincoln responded by stating that, "I am not, nor ever have been, in favor of bringing about in any way the social and political equality of the white and black races ... I am not nor ever have been in favor of making voters or jurors of Negroes, nor of qualifying them to hold office, nor to intermarry with white people; and I will say in addition to this that there is a physical difference between the white and black races which I believe will forever forbid the two races from living together on terms of social and political equality. And inasmuch as they cannot so live, while they do remain together there must be a position of superior and inferior, and I as much as any other man am in favor of having the superior position assigned to the white race."

Second, Abe didn't have some compassionate, bleeding heart for the oppression of Black people. While it is true that in certain instances he can be cited as opposing slavery, he also was explicitly not an abolitionist. His opposition to slavery did not extend to abolishing it as an institution in Amerika. Despite what we're led to believe, destroying slavery was not his initial intent for the civil war. Lincoln's primary aim for the civil war was to keep Amerika whole. When the Confederate states rebelled and threatened to secede from the union, old honest Abe got to work trying to hold Amerika together. He clearly expresses this in a letter he wrote to his friends in which he states, "If I could save the Union without freeing any slave, I would do it, and if I could save it by freeing all the slaves I would do it; and if I could save it by freeing some and leaving others alone, I would also do that."

Let's keep in mind that these statements were officially documented as coming from the same man who signed the Fugitive Slave Act into law. The law that made it legal for slave owners to retrieve slaves that had successfully runaway and fled to the North and bring them back into slavery. This is also the same man who committed the largest mass execution in Amerikan history when he commuted the sentences of 264 out of 303 Dakota men. 38 were left to hang in Mankato, Minnesota in 1862.

It seems the more we dig into Abraham Lincoln, the more we find out just how badly we've all been lied to. Unfortunately, there's more. Being known as the man who freed the slaves provided quite a few opportunities to continue white supremacy. By portraying Black people as too weak and docile to facilitate their own liberation, white supremacy is able to simultaneously reinforce the ridiculous idea that Black people needed a white person to save them along with rewriting history to make it appear as though slavery ended due to the North's victory in the civil war. Both are absurdly incorrect. Contrary to popular belief, Black people did not passively and fearfully accept their conditions under chattel slavery. By and large they were not the obedient, pathetic slaves who only pursued freedom by escaping to the north as we're so often taught. The amount of slave rebellions that occurred throughout the history of chattel slavery in Amerika has been both grossly under reported and purposely re-branded in order to deter Black people away from their true history. Of course, they taught about Nat Turner and maybe even in some cases John Brown. Make no mistake, both men were heroes who deserve to be re-membered and celebrated for their efforts. But in essence, those were failed rebellions. Both Nat Turner and John Brown were defeated, cap-tured and executed with no change in the conditions of slavery at the time. Why have we not been taught about the successful rebellions like the Gullah wars, The Maroons, or Toussaint Louverture? The Gul-lah/Geechee people are Black people in South Carolina and Georgia who were able to stay connected to their African roots and culture. From 1739 to 1858, the Gullahs maintained their freedom through a series of rebel-lions, battles, insurrections, and organization with other enslaved Black people.

Beginning with the Stono rebellion, the Gullahs eventually migrated south to Florida where they established autonomous settlements for Black people to live free and train in combat in order to defend their free-dom. As they began to secure their freedom, they then began to ally with Native Americans who were fighting against our colonialism. Any time a Gullah warrior was captured and sold into slavery, the warrior would quickly agitate the other enslaved Black people and cause uprisings on the plantations.

The Gullah's arch nemesis, Andrew Jackson, was particularly brutal with his involvement in these wars. He had captured Gullah warriors tor-tured and decapitated before placing their heads on pikes as an example to other Gullah rebels. After losing the battle of Suwanee, he had Gullah and Native women and children beaten, raped, and killed. He falsely claimed to win battles that were decisive victories for the Gullah people. He mislabeled defeats as massacres so as to mislead his superiors and the public into believing these were savages that he was dealing with instead of a superior military force.

Yet and still, these wars intensified which led to the deaths of hun-dreds of thousands of Union soldiers. This eventually culminated into pressuring the North to end slavery. Lincoln signed the emancipation proclamation as a publicity stunt to cover up the fact that the Gullah people had fought, won, and kept their freedom on their own. Later, these wars were renamed the Seminole wars to mislead us into believing that these conflicts were with Natives and separate from the issues surrounding slavery. What is so often omitted from the history books is that the Natives fighting against our genocidal colonialism allied with the Gullah people to make up the Seminole tribe. There was no such tribe named the Seminoles in traditional Native America before we came and instituted chattel slavery. The Seminoles only became a tribe after we got here. The word Seminole literally translates to "runaway". Similarly, the word "maroon" used in the Caribbean literally means "fugitive".

What many of us fail to understand is that the end of chattel slavery did not mean the end of its effects. It is impossible to institutionalize a system as barbaric and traumatic as race-based chattel slavery without that institution having resounding repercussions throughout history. When you spend your whole life doing back breaking labor for 14, 15, 16 hours a day, you would think, by the end of your life, you should have something to show for all that hard work. And you should be able to pass that down to your kids. Well, Black people spent 400 years doing just that, except, it was the people who kidnapped them, tortured them, whipped them, raped them, and forced them to do that work who were the ones with something to show for those long laboring days. The fortunes that were amassed by slave labor were never returned to the people it rightfully belonged to; the ones who did the work. And, in fact, after the abolition of chattel slavery, former slave owners were awarded reparations for each slave they were forced to give up. Furthermore, the formerly enslaved people were promised 40 acres of land and a mule as compensation for their centuries of enduring the brutality and terrorism of forced, unpaid labor only to never see the fulfillment of that compensation.

Therefore, it is imperative to understand that the denial for reparations the Black people for chattel slavery is the same as admitting to the belief that slavery is an acceptable economic institution. Either you support reparations, or you support slavery. Moreover, since Black people's free, forced labor was no longer an option, and their promised compensation was never delivered, they were left to fend for themselves in a hostile land that now hated them.

But that's just what they did. Black people began building up their own communities together. Almost instinctively, they returned to their pre-slavery roots and worked together to build vibrant, thriving communities with cooperative economics and necessary societal professionals like doctors, nurses, lawyers, mail people, garbage people, construction workers, etc. These communities began cropping up all over Amerika. Slocum, Texas; Rosewood, Florida; New Orleans, Louisiana; Colfax, Louisiana; Springfield, Illinois; Camila, Georgia; Memphis, Tennessee, and Tulsa, Oklahoma just to name a few. Black people did in these communities what Black people have been doing for centuries, flourishing in the face of adversity. If Abraham Lincoln really wanted to free the slaves, he would have used his shrewd political mind to conceive some type of social and economic transitional strategy for Black people following the emancipation proclamation. Instead, Black people did it all for themselves, and they did it well by building these communities and making them thrive.

Of course, however, this upset white people which led to another 150 years of Black massacres. Every aforementioned city, as well as many others not mentioned, faced the terrorism of white people who could not stand to see Black people doing so well for themselves that we literally invaded these communities, usually dressed in traditional KKK robes and police uniform, with the sole purpose of destroying them. Burning, looting, rioting, and murdering men, women, and children. Notably one of the most devastating Black massacres was in 1921 when Tulsa, Oklahoma, otherwise known as Black Wall Street as it was then the wealthiest Black community in the U.S., was invaded by mobs of white people who had been armed and deputized by city officials destroyed more than 35 square blocks attacking residents and businesses. In all, more than 800 people were seriously injured, and while 39 deaths have been officially confirmed, estimates place the total death toll around 300. As previously mentioned, this was not an isolated incident. This happened all across the United States. Wherever Black people went to live and be free, white people, to one degree or another, brutalized, terrorized, bullied, displaced, and inflicted violence upon them.

In 1820s New York, another such community known as Seneca Village was a predominantly Black community full of life, love, and communal bonds. Made of mostly free Black people and a few Irish, Seneca Village was established for them to escape the racist atmosphere of Manhattan as well as affording them the chance to own land. During the 1820s, if Black men owned land, they were allowed to vote. Then, using the law of eminent domain, the city uprooted Seneca Village, displaced the entire community effectively stripping Black men of their voting rights to build what is now known as Central Park.

These are just a few of the truths and realities that were either changed or omitted from the history books and class lessons. It would seem that each one of them was either altered or left out specifically to mislead people away from certain facts due to the common inspiration potential that runs through them all. So, why is history in school taught from European origins if history itself far predates Europe? The answer seems quite clear. In any event, the fact remains that Black and Native people are under no obligation to forgive us for the repugnant, grotesque, and malevolent atrocities we've committed against them for the past 600 years. However, if they choose to, not only should we count our blessings but, we also need to change the systems our ancestors put in place that keep our boots on the backs of their necks, lest they decide to rescind that forgiveness and instead opt for revenge, which they would be well within their right to do.

Chapter 10
Police and the (In)Justice System

Most people take police as a given, as a social necessity and inevitability. It seems from birth we're inundated with propaganda from school, media, music, mentors and even each other that is designed to condition us with the idea that police are on our side. We're taught to believe that they are the good guys. That they look out for us. That they are public servants here to protect and serve society to keep it safe. As kids we're often told that if we're in trouble and cannot find our parents, that we should find a police officer to help. The D.A.R.E. program used police as representatives against the dangers of drugs and usually demonized other members of society to do so. Placing police in opposition to low level drug pushers, they implied that life will be a series of experiences that put us face-to-face with either good or evil and that police were the good guys.

However, if we take a closer look at the history of police, we can see that this mentality is a direct contradiction to both the establishment and development of police, as well as the economic and legal constructs of our society that dictate police operation. Some may even find this difficult to imagine, but what if police are not really here to serve and protect? What if they are not even really a social necessity? Is it possible that enforcing racism and classism are the only reason police exist at all? What if there were not only more viable, but also more civil and humane alternatives to police, prisons, judges, courts, prosecutors and the entire misnamed justice system?

First, let's understand that the topic of police, police brutality, police murder, and the very oppressive nature of the entire so-called justice system goes well beyond the "bad-apple" theory. The bad-apple theory suggests that the problem with police is limited to the personal conduct of a few individual officers. But the stories we hear in the news and the entire catalyst for the Black Lives Matter movement, as well as the civil rights movement and the Black Power movement is not at all limited to just a few "bad cops". Let's be perfectly clear that even if the police were never rude or abusive or never murdered another Black person ever again, they would still be socially problematic. This will become clearer by the end of the chapter.

Second, let's take a look at the origins of police, specifically the ones in the U.S. The United States is essentially divided into the north and the south by the Mason-Dixon line. The Mason-Dixon line can be considered the line that divided the North and the South in the Amerikan Civil War. Although the model of police in the US follows the "Peelers" who were the first police force in England to take its modern shape in 1829, the police in the US come from one of two places. North of the Mason-Dixon line, police originated as protectors for the wealthy, ruling class. Their job was to protect the profits and power of the land and business owners against the people who worked on the land and in factories. Their job was to use violence and intimidation to prevent factory, plant, mill, dock, and other employees, from organizing to fight for better wages and working conditions. Things like the 40-hour work week, the minimum wage, child labor laws, weekends, holidays, sick days, and unions were fought for by the workers amid an environment of extremely violent repression by the state who employed police to protect the interests – i.e. the profits - of the wealthy. Although the majority of the workers who faced the violence from police in the North were white, it must be recognized that at that time, nearly every Black person who lived in the North faced this violence because they were also part of the working class. Not all the people who faced the violence were Black, but all the Black people faced the violence.

South of the Mason-Dixon line, police originate from the slave catchers. The police are directly descended from the men who would ride around the plantations and patrolling the streets on horses, carrying guns, wearing badges that read "slave patrol" and captured run-away slaves. It was the job of police to hunt, capture, and return the enslaved men, women, and children who attempted to escape their brutal bondage. And they were afforded a very liberal policy on violence to do it.

It is with this history that it becomes blatantly obvious just why the institution of police was created. In both the north and the south, the police were designed and implemented with the sole purpose of protecting the interests – that is, the profits – of those who were in power. After all, profits were the source of their power. And in Amerika, in one way or another, Black people have always been the source of profit. In order to maintain this power differential, the police were afforded a monopoly on authority and violence in order to prevent the dissent of everyone else who suffered from this unequal distribution of power. The more the working class and enslaved people suffered at the hands of those who controlled their lives, the more upset they would become. The more upset the working class and the enslaved people would become, the more violently police would respond. This was the beginning of institutional and systemic racism. It is from these social implementations that we as a society grew from.

Nevertheless, police are just a part of a bigger whole. They are only one aspect of a system that is as violent and racist in its origins as the police. We've all heard the happy ending fairy tale about the 13th amendment and the so-called abolition of slavery. However, let's forget everything the teachers and public school system taught us for a moment and do our own research. If we take a look at the state of our so-called justice system today, it poses a strong challenge to this claim that slavery actually ended. First of all, we're told that Abraham Lincoln signed the emancipation proclamation which led to the ratification of the 13th amendment to the U.S. constitution which formally and officially abolishes slavery in the U.S. However, if we were to actually read what the 13th amendment says we would realize the 13th amendment explicitly states that "... slavery shall not exist *EXCEPT FOR PUNISHMENT OF A CRIME.*" If we fast forward to the 21st century, we see that despite being only 5% of the world's population, Amerika has over 25% of the world's prison population. In fact, not only does Amerika have more people in prison than any other country in the world but, we actually have more people in prison than has ever been in history by any other empire.

As if that wasn't sickening enough, consider the demographic of the people in prison. Despite being only 13-14% of Amerika's whole population, over 60% of the people in prison are Black. In fact, there are more Black men in prison today than were enslaved in 1856. Black women are the fastest growing demographic for incarceration. In virtually every case, the prisoner comes from a working-class background. This seems like a lot more than a coincidence, especially considering that in 2014 the private prison industry alone recorded profits of $629 million. Wait, $629 million made from the free forced labor of black, brown and poor people...? Why that sounds like slavery! However, what many people do not know is that it isn't just private prisons that are for profit institutions. All prisons are for profit. In prison, if you don't work, you don't survive. The food that is provided is barely edible let alone enough to live on. All personal effects including toilet tissue, toothpaste, toothbrushes, menstrual products for women, deodorant, chap stick, pillows, sheets, soap, supplementary food, and all else must be bought from the commissary with your own money. Unless you have people outside regularly putting money on your books, the only way to survive is to work.

With all that being said, we must also understand that work in prison is not the same as work in the rest of Amerika. The prisons contract with private businesses to use their inmates for labor. Companies like Victoria's Secret, Target, Cargill, major Universities, and many others have been reported to use prison labor. They pay these inmates anywhere from 25 cents an hour to 94 cents a day to manufacture the products that they sell to you for the same price as if they had been made by union workers.

The slave wages earned by the inmates is then used to purchase basic everyday necessities. This does not include leisure or nutritional rations. The items that inmates need to purchase are sold at roughly the same price that we purchase them for. However, this weighs much harder on the inmates considering that on average, each inmate spends over $1000 a year at the commissary, yet only make anywhere between $180 to $660 a year. This means that the money goes right back to the prison. Commissary sales gross over $1 billion a year. And the discrepancy between earned wages and necessary spending? Well... that's usually made up by things like using torn up socks or sheets as toilet tissue only to be washed and reused, living in abject filth for not being able to afford household cleaners, and a lack of contact with loved ones for not being able to afford the astronomically outrageous price for phone calls.

Now we have to take into account that every single person in prison was first taken into custody by police. In 2005, the Supreme Court ruled that police are under no legal obligation to "serve and protect." Their only job function is to enforce the law. It must also be understood that this ruling only served to reaffirm what was already understood and practiced by law enforcement. It did not change anything in police job operation or description.

Apparently, these laws are much more bloodthirsty than we're led to believe because in Amerika, a black person is killed by police every 21 hours. Evidently, they can't even wait a full day before getting back out there to ethnically cleanse the streets. In 2012, Amerikans were 8 times more likely to be killed by a cop than a terrorist (I personally don't see the difference between the two). However, in 2015, those odds skyrocketed to 55 times more likely!!! Between 2010 and 2012, about 1.5 per 1 million white males aged 15 – 19 were killed by police. In the same time frame and age bracket, over 31 per 1 million black males were killed by police. That's almost 30 times more young Black men killed by police than young white men. As if those numbers didn't paint a gruesome enough picture, the overall population demographic make-up illustrates an even more vivid picture of institutionalized racism. There are only about 42 million black people in the U.S. contrasted by over 200 million white people in the U.S. Still, that's just scratching the surface of institutionalized racism, however, it becomes obvious that the role of police in the black community has never been what we were told it is. In fact, all we have to do test it against reason. Every neighborhood in Amerika that has the highest crime rate will invariably be a Black community created by racist economic practices that rob and deprive these communities of resources. These communities will also concurrently be the most saturated with police presence. If police were at all effective or necessary, shouldn't these neighborhoods have the lowest crime rates?

What's happening is that society has caused us to confuse occupation with character. The way our society is structured, many of us are conditioned to believe that our occupation is an element of our identity. The ubiquity and frequency with which this concept arises in our everyday thought process is enough to automatically ingrain it within our psyche.

Often times, when we meet new people, our occupation is one of the first—if not the very first—pieces of information we share about ourselves. It's not out of the ordinary to offer what our vocation may be as an inroad for others to gain more insight about who we are as a person. But while it is possible for our jobs to indeed be indicative of certain characteristics that make up our identity, the occupation itself stands alone independently of who we are as a person. We would be who are regardless of what work we did to make money. It is just as possible to have a scientific, analytical mind and be a janitor as it is to have a scientific, analytical mind and be a doctor. It is just as possible to be caring and empathetic while waiting tables as it is to be caring and empathetic while being a nurse.

Thus, the assertion that there is no such thing as a good cop is not a personal indictment. It isn't an inherent onslaught against the personal identity or character of anyone. It is a summary analysis of the occupation itself. So, when it's said that there's no such thing as a good cop, it doesn't mean there aren't good people who then become cops. However, if someone with a badge does a good thing, that's them being a good person—not being a good cop. You don't need a badge to do good deeds. You do need a badge to enforce an unequal distribution of power.

With all of that said, we also have to remember that there is a big difference between being a good person and being a nice person. Often times, we tend to mistake someone who is being nice as someone who is being good. So ultimately, becoming a cop is a choice. Thus, due to the nature and purpose of the occupation, it is a choice that undermines any goodness that may have otherwise existed, current or past. Being a good person in the past or off the job does not exempt or excuse the choice to enforce oppression. And it is more likely that they're a nice person rather than a good person.

The entire existence of police is to ensure that people comply and conduct their lives within the confines of what the law says is acceptable, and that's the only purpose they have ever served. At first, this sounds noble and respectable enough until we remember that chattel slavery was the law. Apartheid was the law. The holocaust was the law. The Cambodian killing fields were the law. The Armenian genocide was the law.

Conversely, escaping and helping enslaved people escape was against the law. Hiding Jews was a criminal offense. Black people were arrested for using the same restrooms and water fountains as white people. The law is not a basis for justice, democracy, or morality. It is a basis for power. And it is enforced solely to protect those who have it from those who don't.

Allow me to offer an analogy. See if you can spot the similarities. During the reign of the Third Reich in Nazi Germany, a man by the name Adolf Eichmann was tasked with, among other things, making sure that the trains running to and from the Auschwitz concentration camp ran on their scheduled time. Essentially, what this means is that it was Eichmann's job to ensure that thousands of innocent Jewish people were in a state-determined place at a state determined time to meet an eventual state-determined death.

In the 1960s, a psychologist named Hanna Arendt did a case study on Adolf Eichmann. Later, Dr. Aredesnt wrote a book on her case study which she entitled "The Banality of Evil." Dr. Aredesnt gave this title to her book because in her case study, what she found out was that by every other account, Adolf Eichmann was just a regular, average guy. He was married, he had children, his children went to school, he owned a house, he paid bills, mowed the lawn on Saturdays, went to church on Sundays, and he had a career. It just so happened that his career was a part of a bigger whole. A mechanism within a system that was designed to keep Jewish people oppressed and favor white people of Germanic descent.

In fact, Dr. Aredesnt discovered that Adolf Eichmann didn't even harbor any particular disdain for Jewish people. As I turned out, Adolf Eichmann—like most of us—was just "doing his job." The virtue of "doing one's duty", "following orders", or "respecting your superiors" by blindly obeying their commands is non-existent. There is no honor in just doing your job without questioning the actions that doing your job requires. Historian Howard Zinn said, "Historically, the most terrible things - war, genocide, and slavery - have resulted not from disobedience, but from obedience." The greatest atrocities of human history have been caused not by people disobeying the law but by people following and enforcing it. The argument that "I'm just trying to do my job" is not a valid excuse for refusing to think critically. Obedience to policy is not justification for neglecting to use your own judgement. Following the rules is not more moral than thinking for yourself, using your own discretion, and being critical of the rules you're required to follow and enforce. Failing to objectively analyze your job and its relationship to society through a lens that validates more than just one side is not excused by your efforts to perform that job in whatever way gets the most praise from your superiors. Martin Luther King, Jr said, "... one has a moral responsibility to disobey unjust laws." That moral responsibility applies just as much to enforcing unjust laws. Being a "good cop" is akin to being a "good dog". Every single cop, corrections officer, parole officer, prosecutor, politician, prison warden, judge, or any other agent of the Amerikan justice system needs to understand that they will go down in the history books right next to every rank-and-file Nazi. Just the same, anyone who supports, advocates, or condones these institutions is an automatic racist.

As we have seen, the police do not protect and serve the people of the communities they occupy. The police occupy these communities to ensure that the power stays out of these communities. Power is obtained through capital. More money equals more power. The communities that have the most police presence are the ones that generate the most money. However, it is because of this police presence that the communities which generate the most money are the same ones with the least power. This is because the laws are established to favor the business owners, company tycoons, and captains of industry who exploit the labor of these communities by taking the profits that are accumulated through the labor of the people who live in these communities. The economic laws and accepted socio-political standards outline a framework for business operation that grant the people who do the actual, physical producing a mere fraction of the total money that comes from the sale of whatever is produced. The rest goes into the hands of the company's upper echelons who do the least work. As we have also seen, it has been explicitly established by the highest court in the land that the job of police is to, in fact, enforce the law thereby effectively keeping the money through which power is obtained, away from those to whom it rightfully belongs. Therefore, it stands to reason that the existence of a police force is inherently racist. Furthermore, it is a racist institution that is part of a larger social and economic arrangement with the sole purpose of reinforcing and maintaining the continuation of itself. Anytime we defend, support, apologize or play devil's advocate for police, we are affirming and upholding the same racist beliefs that birthed police in the first place.

Chapter 11
Gentrifying Everything

Earlier in the book we discussed the racist nature of cultural appropriation. The phenomenon and process of gentrification began entirely separate from cultural appropriation. However, the evolution of gentrification has now extended its reach far beyond its original development of forcing poor, mainly Black people into neighborhoods where poverty is concentrated, to the point where gentrification can often times look very similar to cultural appropriation. Usually, when we talk about gentrification, we think of large, wealthy, nameless, faceless, real estate and property developing corporations buying up land, homes, and shops at a lower cost due to the location in impoverished neighborhoods. Then they renovate and rehab those properties to turn around and sell them at a higher profit which raises property taxes, attracts wealthier buyers to purchase the properties from the developers and results in displacing the impoverished people who that neighborhood originally belonged to. However, because capitalism is where racism gets its power from and it is also the economic basis for gentrification, it means that the entire concept of gentrification is both racist and classist which negatively effects primarily Black people and benefits white people. Therefore, the concept of gentrification can be thought of as extending far beyond just the physical displacement of Black people for the benefit of white people. It can also be thought of as the limitation of access to interests, lifestyles and healthy practices at the detriment of Black people and other people of color for the benefit of white people.

The gentrification of poor Black and brown neighborhoods is only the beginning. At first, the condemned house down the block, the closed down business up the street, or maybe even your own apartment building start getting some much-needed renovations and upgrades. Then you start to notice a few extra Black Lives Matter yard signs and bumper stickers here and there. Next you notice your neighbors are gone and people who were never in your neighborhood before are now showing up everywhere. Then it hits you. Those Black Lives Matter signs have replaced actual Black lives. And now, the neighborhood feels more pretentious and exclusive. This is how we begin to gentrify other aspects of life.

Through the attitudes of exclusion and elitism that we attach to these lifestyles and practices, we create an unwelcoming and judgmental atmosphere to the detriment of Black and other people of color. Many of the practices, lifestyles, and interests that have either been developed in the west or been adopted from other cultures and absorbed into ours eventually come to be known in the Black community and other communities of color as "white people shit". This perception of "white people shit" has come to be used in many different communities as a way to inform the person being accused of doing "white people shit" that what they are doing is lame, gross, unnecessarily dangerous, inexplicably weird, or some other negative observational assessment of their behavior. However, the negative connotation associated with the phrase "white people shit" is not a fault or even a reflection of Black people's over all attitude towards white people. Instead, the use of this phrase is a result of the way that white people have taken over and essentially culturally monopolized these interests, lifestyles and practices.

One of the most prominent lifestyles that we gentrify is self-care. The concept of caring for our own mental and emotional health is one that has been around for many millennia in many different cultures. In one way or another, throughout history, humans have practiced taking care of our mental and emotional health through things like healthy diets, therapy, yoga, and meditation. A healthy diet was just a natural part of our everyday lives. Sustaining ourselves by what nature provided for us naturally is about the healthiest diet humans can achieve. Granted, Black people were probably using a lot more seasoning and spices on their foods but otherwise, our diets were relatively similar and mutually healthy. Both Black and white healers were using foods as a means for curing diseases. Then the agricultural revolution that began in 17th century Britain (a decidedly white empire), the rise of chattel slavery and overall racism, food started to become as much a source of disease as it was a source for remedy. With the invention of food processing in order to mass produce foods which would increase profits and preservatives to maintain a longer shelf life - also to maximize profits, food started to become a source for a litany of health problems. High blood pressure from processed salt, diabetes, renal failure and tooth decay from processed sugar, heart failure and clogged arteries from trans and saturated fats.

Of course, with chattel slavery in the south and the enforcement of a superiority complex by whites in the north, the diets of Black people became vastly different from that of white people. With all the garbage that Black people were forced to be subjected to, it was inevitable that their health would begin to deteriorate. This deterioration was only accelerated by the way they had to prepare the food in order to make it even reasonably close to suitable for human consumption. Combined with the right seasoning, obscene amounts of salt, boiling in fats, deep frying and the like made pig intestines, neck bones, hamhocks, and chicken gizzards all edible. Fortunately, making food delicious is a skill that Black people have had for centuries before chattel slavery. Making inedible food not only edible but, actually delicious was bound to happen. But the ability to make magic flavors with seasoning can only take you so far when the only food you have to flavor can kill you. Over time the tastes of Black people adapted to what they had access to which were then handed down from generation to generation. Now, some of the food that's the most dangerous for humans have become a staple in the Black community diet. And some of the food that's the healthiest for humans have become known as white people food. Not necessarily by reason of health, however.

The food that's the healthiest has become known as white people food for two reasons. The first is because we have no clue how to prepare it. Healthy food could be just as delicious as soul food if only we would use some seasoning and spices. Nevertheless, and perhaps more importantly, foods that tend to be healthier are more expensive, harder to access, and come attached with an attitude of superiority and elitism. Mostly stocked in grocery stores located in predominantly white neighborhoods, these foods are roughly double the cost of what their unhealthier counterparts are. These foods are also marketed specifically to people who tend to exude an attitude of entitlement to the exclusivity of health food simply based on their economic status. The pretentious, bougie attitude that rich white people attach to health food is one that seems designed to repel Black and poor people away from a healthier diet. And if that doesn't work, the high prices and lack of flavor sure will.

Only within the past 50 years or so has the importance of mental and emotional health began to emerge in society as a necessary part of everyday life. However, before chattel slavery and the colonization of Africa, taking care of one's own mental and emotional health were common practice among Black people. It was a usual tribal occurrence in Africa for younger generations to seek out the wisdom and knowledge of the elders to help guide them through life. In the Caribbean, the existence of therapists in the community was as normal as a doctor or teacher. In fact, in the process of white people's mission to demonize both Black culture and mental health, they began to use derogatory terms in reference to Caribbean therapists. Calling them "witch doctors" and "head shrinkers" to make them seem scarier, more evil and more dangerous. This is where the term "shrink" in reference to a therapist originates. The entire concept of caring for one's mental and emotional health began with Black people. With the onset of chattel slavery and European colonization of Africa however, the stigma white people attached to mental and emotional health was that it was either a sign of weakness or of feeble mindedness; or both.

Already subjected to the social perception of mental inferiority by white people, Black people began to adopt this same rationale towards mental and emotional health. It became a sign of weakness and a cause for ridicule in the Black community for one to seek out therapy, medication, and treatment for mental and emotional health issues. But, now that white people have started to realize the benefits and necessity of mental and emotional health treatment, we've made it all but completely inaccessible to the two groups of people that have the most trauma. And they have it because of us! We demonized the cultural practice of taking care of mental and emotional health which was originally a staple in Black and Native communities. We passed on the attitude that a therapeutic social practice which was a benefit for both the individual and the community is weak and evil, then started to adopt the practice ourselves once we realized how beneficial it is, all while causing them the most deplorable human suffering the world has ever seen. Now we keep it away from the people who need it the most by placing a majority of mental health clinics, individual therapists, and psychiatrists out in the suburbs in predominantly white communities. We charge obscene amounts of money for their services which are usually covered by health insurance except we make obtaining health insurance the most difficult for Black, Brown, Native, and poor people.

Jazz music began in the early 1910s in New Orleans, Louisiana. As a part of Black culture, Jazz grew as a hybrid between the older blues of the south and the modern ragtime music that was popular at the time. Initially, jazz was improvised by musicians as music for Black people to dance to. As jazz started to spread throughout the U.S., these new sounds which used what are called "bent" or "blue" notes that are not found on the traditional music scale started to scare and appall the mostly conservative white population of the U.S. True to form, white people began to demonize jazz music and jazz musicians. We labeled the artists as criminals and junkies. We stigmatized the music as immoral and evil. Jazz concerts and dance halls became taboo where no respectable white person would be caught dead but, many couldn't stay away from. The allure of pulsating rhythms, the attraction to creative genius, and of course the impulse to indulge in whatever society tells you is bad for you all proved to be too much for many white folks to resist. Under cover of night, many white people would venture out incognito to partake in a culture that their soul just couldn't deny. Over time, more and more white people began to crave the experience of culture through jazz music. So much so that white people even began to perform it. Jazz was now becoming acceptable in mainstream society. It has been stolen out of the slums and poverty of New Orleans where it was invented as a culture for spiritual survival and brought to the upscale night clubs and upper-class venues of metropolitan nightlife. It's become a means for making white people feel deep and cultured because we live in a society that has no culture. We even pretend to like bad jazz music just to give off the impression that we're sophisticated enough to justify how pretentious and exclusive we've made it. The human spirit craves culture. It needs it. In attempting to separate Black people from the culture of their ancestors, our racism managed to separate from our own culture. Now, the only culture we have is stealing other cultures. But because white people commodify everything, profit becomes the main motive for everything we do, including stealing culture. So, our process for stealing culture includes making it as classist as possible. Through the attitudes and price tags that we've attached to certain cultural staples, gentrification of these cultural elements was inevitable when people with no culture who only value greed came into contact with them. One of the most hidden, unrealized, and self-destructive aspects of demonizing other cultures and attempting to inferiorize them is that we end up with a soulless, unsubstantial culture of our own.

Chapter 12
Karen

You know those people at work who act like your supervisor even though they aren't? That's a "Karen". The person who acts like a supervisor even outside of work. The person who's got her nose in everyone else's business except her own. The person who instigates a confrontation and then plays the victim when the outcome doesn't go their way. Like the younger siblings who hits the older one and then cries to mommy when the older one stands up for themselves. Those are the "Karen" types. The name "Karen" is the quintessential, suburban soccer mom, white woman name. As such, the term "Karen" was adopted as a colloquialism that has come to refer to someone who displays behaviors that are typical of white women on relation to Black people. Behaviors such as unwarranted defensiveness, asserting baseless accusations, assuming the role of an authority figure in situations that neither require one nor qualify her to be one, and all of the above-mentioned situations involving Black people, are typical "Karen" behaviors. Although these behaviors are not exclusive to white women, they are the most prevalent in white women. Their prevalence in white women stems from their use against Black people. When white women feel threatened by Black people, they have a tendency to follow this particular pattern of behaviors. However, two aspects of this perceived threat need to be recognized. First is that the racism implied by this pattern of behaviors is a result of the racism that is implied by the perceived threat. If the racism were not present in the person who felt threatened, then the racist actions that followed would also, most likely, not occur. It is the perceived threat that itself is racist. The actions that follow are how that racism is enforced. Second is that the perceived threat is itself dynamic. While there is no objective threat actually present, a Karen may feel, or claim to feel threatened for a few different reasons. They may feel a non-existent threat to their safety, or, as in many of the more recent cases, they may feel a threat to what they believe is their superiority. This latter reasoning is the most likely of the two.

Ever since white people have controlled society, white women have been preying on Black people's autonomy and free will. Either by appealing to white men's sense of superiority and dominance to control Black people by proxy or by causing conflict and then influencing public opinion by pretending to be the victim, white women have sought to control the actions and behaviors of Black people through manipulating situations and perceptions. Initiating conflict and then appealing to a higher authority while portraying innocence allows white women to manipulate situations through threat of violence which would be asserted by an agent of white women on her behalf. Doing so while playing the victim in front of a large group of people allows white women to control Black people through threat of ridicule and humiliation. Since physical intimidation is rarely possible, Karen types have figured out more cunning ways to use the monopoly that white society has on violence to establish a sense of control and dominance over Black people.

Anytime a Black person behaves in a way that white women find unacceptable, or they are in a place that white women do not want them to be in, this manipulative and abusive behavior arises. Dehumanizing Black people through causing conflict with them and then playing the victim by acting innocent and violated in order to ensure the conflict goes ends in their favor has always been a go-to tactic for white women in order to establish a sense of control and dominance. Either way, both perceptions stem from racists beliefs.

The pattern of behavior that follows is almost always an appeal to authority; usually calling the police. In some instances, they may involve the manager of an establishment or a more intimidating friend but, usually it's the police. The historical relationship between police and Black people offers "Karen" types the feeling of support they need to reinforce their sense of dominance and control. Unfortunately, due to the nature of this relationship between police and Black people, it often works.

It should be understood that people are going to act how they feel. If someone wants to act like a manager without the endowment of the title, then that's their business. It should be dealt with according to however is seen fit. However, when those types of interactions involve the perception or implication of a superior/inferior or dominant/subordinate relationship between a white person and a Black person, the issue of racism automatically arises. Therefore, when police become involved, they automatically become the arbiters and enforcers for white supremacy. The attitude of superiority displayed by the "Karen" type as well as any attempt to reinforce the attitude through an assertion of power is essentially the "Karen" type's way of reestablishing what we as white people consider to homeostasis. We feel that if a Black person is doing something or is present somewhere that we don't think they should be, we find any source of power that we can resort to in order to return to our sense of social balance and harmony. What seems to escape our comprehension is that what we consider to be balance and harmony isn't at all balanced and harmonious. There is no social or economic equilibrium between white and Black people. But since we fail to understand that any time a Black person begins to act as an equal to white people, there's always a "Karen" around who resorts to her go-to tactic as an attempt to restore the status quo by exerting power however she can.

The fact that white women feel threatened, for whatever reason, by Black people who are simply just trying to live their lives is how the racism of the "Karen" manifests. What "Karen" types need to understand is that we are not in charge of Black people. We are not their supervisors, managers, overseers, or bosses. And the police are not customer service for us anytime a Black person is or isn't doing what we think they should or shouldn't be doing. Grilling in a restricted area? They're not hurting you. And you most likely wouldn't be so concerned about it if they weren't Black. Mind your business. Selling water without a permit? You are not the city's manager. Either buy some water or shut up and move on. You see a Black person with an IPhone? Assume its theirs. Or better yet, stop paying so much attention to Black people when they're just trying to go about their day. You. Are not. In charge. And Black people do not owe you a damn thing.

Chapter 13
Denial

There's an old fairy tale called "The Emperor's New Clothes". It goes like this. The emperor of a city loves fine clothing. One day, two men arrive in the city claiming to be the best weavers in the world. They claim to make the finest clothes which are also magical and, as such, are invisible to anyone who is stupid. The emperor is excited and pays the two men a lot of money to make him some new clothes. The two men are then brought into an empty room where they pretended to weave the clothing with empty looms. The emperor sends some of his back men to check on the work the two men are doing. When the Emperor's men realize they see nothing, they do not want to admit it for fear of being thought to be stupid and incompetent. So, the Emperor's men lie to the emperor, saying how the clothing was magnificent. The clothing is brought to the emperor on the day of a great procession. The emperor does not see the clothing either, but he, too, did not want to admit it for fear being thought stupid. So, he agrees that the clothing is exquisite. After being dressed in the invisible garments, the emperor marches in the procession in front of his entire kingdom. Everyone in the kingdom sees the emperor without clothes, but for fear of being accused of being stupid, they all praise the emperor's fine clothing. Finally, a child says, "But he doesn't have anything on!" Everyone realizes that if an innocent child is saying this, then it must be true. Everyone begins to agree and realize that the emperor is not wearing any clothes.

Malcolm X said, "If you stick a knife in my back nine inches and pull it out six inches, there's no progress. If you pull it all the way out that's not progress. Progress is healing the wound that the blow made. And they haven't even pulled the knife out much less heal the wound. They won't even admit the knife is there." White Amerika won't even admit the knife we keep in the back of Black, Brown, and Native people is there, let alone attempt to pull it out. What it boils down to is fear. Most of you have already turned your nose up and rejected any amount of validity this book may have to your life. Once you read the title, your ego got so hurt at such an offensive assertion and scared that you might be equated to a member of the KKK that you immediately decided this book couldn't possibly apply to you. That is to be expected. By and large, white people will do anything to keep from being called racist, except not be racist. We're more concerned with not being called racist than we are with not being racist. If we actually cared about not being racist, we would do more to educate ourselves on racism. And we would start by releasing ourselves from our current understanding of its definition. We hold onto this definition because it keeps us safe. We feel like all we have to do is live our lives in opposition to this definition and then we can be safely counted out as one of the evil, hateful bad people. However, releasing ourselves from our current understanding of racism means that we have to face the very real possibility that we're not as non-racist as we think we are. This prospect is so scary to us that, instead, we take the harder route because it's less frightening. We stagnate our learning, obstruct our growth as humans and hide behind our arrogance. We conclude that what we already understand is good enough and no further learning needs to be undertaken. And we become fine holding onto our racism as long as we're not identified as one.

Not everyone is able to consider that they don't have all the answers. Not everyone is able to learn new things. Not everyone is even willing to. Some people are just so scared that their reality will come crashing down around them if they admit out loud that it is built on fraudulent beliefs rooted in bigotry or ignorance that they'll adopt the most hypocritical belief system just to prevent themselves from having to face that fear. Ironically, this fear is so pervasive that the majority of people who harbor it have developed particular defense mechanisms aimed at maintaining their denial by using some of the very same tactics that addicts use to maintain their addiction.

Intellectualization, rationalization, bullying and hypocrisy are some of the more common schemes we employ to deny our racism. Attempting to offer overly complex explanations and descriptions of modern society while using pretentious and academic language not only helps to confuse and complicate the issue but, it also plays right into our sense of superiority. The use of "post-modern" and "nuanced" as descriptors for contemporary society or trying to apply the historical development of human relationships and social dynamics throughout time is nothing more than an attempt to filter racism through intellectual topics. This filtration of racism convolutes the issue which makes it much easier to explain away and separate ourselves from our personal role in its continuation.

Furthermore, the attempt to draw a distinction between racism, systemic racism, and white supremacy is just petty. Using semantic arguments to try and create differences that don't really exist or adhering to a rigid and stagnant understanding of these concepts only shows just how far we're willing to go to be right instead of putting that effort into making progress both personally and socially.

Additionally, through the use of words like "snowflake", many of us who are in denial about our own racism will accuse others who challenge it of being over-sensitive or weak. This assertion that people who challenge our racism are over-sensitive is a way for us to deny our racism by rejecting responsibility for it. The rejection of this responsibility comes through shifting the focus of attention away from our racism and onto an issue that we can use to make ourselves feel superior. Once our racism is challenged, we push back by posing a counter-challenge to people's ego by attacking their emotional strength. We accuse them of being weak or over-sensitive and try to intimidate them through the fear of ridicule. This intimidation works to minimize the seriousness of our racism and instead, tries to place those who call-out our racism into a vulnerable position. Once they are in that position, the attention is now focused on their emotional vulnerability and away from their challenge to our racism. This tactic is not only textbook bullying but also serves to blind us from the hypocritical irony that these accusations are themselves brought on by our sensitivity to the exposure of our racism.

Other people are scared of the hard work that will inevitably go into rebuilding their reality once they admit that it's weak and unstable. It means they would have to relearn everything they once thought they understood. There are others who are too afraid to consider any viewpoint that differs from their own as being valid because it would mean that they could no longer relate to the world on black and white terms (no pun intended). Some people just don't have the bravery it takes to accept shades of gray.

So, let's take a minute to explore these shades of gray. What we see is just how unoriginal and historically redundant your attitude towards racism in general, as well as your own personal racism really is. There were people who thought that racism ended when chattel slavery ended. They thought that the civil rights movement was as disruptive and immoral as those who think the BLM movement is. These people thought that the civil rights movement was unnecessary because Black people should just be grateful that they aren't enslaved anymore. There were white people who were against the civil rights movement that still didn't consider themselves racist because they weren't out burning crosses and lynching Black people. You don't consider yourself racist because you're not trying to keep Black people from sitting at the front of the bus or voting but you oppose the Black Lives Matter movement and think Colin Kaepernick and LeBron James should just shut up and entertain you. Your claims against your own racism aren't evolved, they're not progressive or civilized or even original. Just because the racism of your time looks different than the racism of you grandparent's time doesn't mean it's any better. It just means that it's adapted to the winds of change. However, on the off chance that your curiosity has managed to overtake your stubborn fears and you have actually made it this far through the book, then there's a few questions that should be asked, but only answered if you're brave enough to be honest. Is it possible that you don't know everything? Is it possible that someone else's point of view could be just as valid as your own? Have you ever been wrong about anything in your life? Could you be wrong about this? Have you ever thought you fully understood something only to find out later that the topic went deeper than you first thought? Have you ever asked your Black friend how they feel about being the only reason you're not racist? Is it worth millions of lives for you to maintain your state of denial? Do you even care?

If you're already the best version of yourself that you are ever going to be, then you should have stopped reading this during the preface. If you already know everything there is to know about racism and still oppose the assertion made in the title of this book, then I have no interest in trying to convince you otherwise. It means that you're okay with being racist and that's just where it stands. You are the emperor in your new clothes. Whether you are brave enough to admit it or not, you're racist, and everyone can see it but you.

Chapter 14
Language

We would never hear someone engage in casual conversation speaking the way they did in 17th century England. However, if we were to listen to someone from 17th century England speaking, we would be able to understand at least the basic premise of what they were saying. This is because even though it is being used differently by two different speakers, the language that is being spoken is still English. This nuance that language is evolutionary is one that so often goes unrealized and unacknowledged. Language evolves over time to suit the overall attitudes and relationships in society. This is true of all modern and ancient languages. It is an undeniable anthropological fact that language changes with the times.

The failure to include the realization that language changes and evolves over time is conveniently used as a way for white supremacy to assert itself. Disavowing this fact provides the perfect opportunity for white people to stay comfortable in our racism without feeling like a racist. By assuming an elitist attitude, we can inflict our racism on both immigrants and citizens of color alike. Anytime we hear an immigrant speaking another language, we can appeal to our sense of patriotism by demanding their assimilation into our society through learning and using the language we use. What we are so often ignorant of is that the U.S. does not have an official language. You know what they speak in Italy? Italian.

You know what they speak in France? French. You what they speak in China? Chinese. Even Chinese has different dialects like Cantonese and Mandarin. But we were never taught about different dialects of the English language in school. We learned that there is only one way to use the English language and anything that deviated from that was considered indicative of stupidity and low class. Incidentally, this just provides further proof that the Amerikan school system is a white supremacist institution.

Ironically, however, the racism demonstrated by white people through linguistic elitism and condescension only tends to apply to immigrants of color. I've never heard a racist insist that someone who is speaking French or German to speak English. I've never heard a white supremacist tell a Russian or a Swede to go back to their country for speaking their language.

Whenever we hear Black people using AAVE we degrade them by correcting words, syntax, and grammar. We condescend them by telling them that certain language they use is improper or incorrect. "Finna isn't a word", "it's ASK, not AXE", and "ain't never is a double negative" are commonly used by white people to make ourselves feel superior to Black people. We make demands to Black people that they speak according to what we deem as acceptable without being able to follow those same rules.

The racism of language grows out of our hypocrisy. We demand that their speech is on par with our expectations yet do not ourselves live up to them. We tell Black people that "finna" isn't a word but use the word "gonna" every day. Both words are contractions, both words are used in predictive or intentional contexts, and neither of them were part of the English vernacular in 17th century England. Yet only one of them is acceptable to the majority of white people who need a reason to look down on Black people. In the early part of the 21st century, white teen girls began constructing their own language out of English by shortening certain words. The interjection of certain words like "totes adorbs" (totally adorable), "obvi" (obviously), and "jelly" (jealous) grew popular among mostly teen, mostly white girls around 2014 - 2015. In the 1950s and 1960s the white youth of suburbia had their own language that today rarely, if ever, gets used in the larger social setting. Words like "hep cat", "groovy", and "square" were popularized and understood by the general high-school age population.

What goes untaught, unrealized, ignored, and completely denied is that in every instance, every word that has ever entered into the English language and adopted by white youth as a way to distinguish their individuality and signal their independence from their parents was either directly invented by or influenced by Black people first. The white people who tell Black people to "use proper English" are the same ones who at one point were using colloquialisms invented by Black people to separate themselves from the generation before them.

Conversely, when it comes to language, white people need to be extremely careful about the language we use with Black people. We cannot always use the same language with Black people that we do with other white people. Based on the history of race relations and the power differential in this country, some of the language that we use with other white people automatically becomes racist when used with Black people.

In the late 2010's, a brief but controversial story in Minneapolis, Minnesota broke about a white barber using certain words to describe the hair of a Black woman who had come to see him for a haircut. The words that he used were innocent enough in general, and personally, I don't believe the barber was being intentionally malicious and may have even been using these descriptions as a poor attempt at building rapport with his new client. However, when put into the context of conversation between a white man and a Black woman, any words that refer to her hair as "wild", "animal" or "tame" instantly become racialized. Historically, white society has done everything it can to damage the relationship that Black people have with their natural hair. By portraying fine, strait, thin hair as the preference and standard for beauty over thick, kinky, course hair, Black women have had to endure centuries of demonizing and shame over what naturally grows out of their head. This is precisely why saying those exact same words to a white woman will likely not have the same psychological effect. White women have not been conditioned with the same beliefs about their hair that Black women have. Using words to describe a Black woman's hair that could be conveyed as anything but positive and uplifting is rooted in the white supremacist idea that white hair is better and prettier than Black hair. This is how it becomes racist.

The purpose of language is to communicate. Whether it be to convey needs, wants, ideas, or intents, the key to language is mutual understanding. When two or more people are able to comprehend what is being communicated and the way that it is being communicated then whatever words are being used are proper and correct. To assert otherwise is just as racist as white people using the "N" word. Furthermore, as white people we have been so reckless and destructive with our language for so long that in order to prevent doing any more harm, we now have to be extra conscious of what we say and who we say it to.

Chapter 15
Systemic

To begin with, let's try to keep in mind that this chapter is all in addition to that of police, prisons, and the so-called justice system which also qualify as systemic racism but, due to their inherently egregious, abysmal, and vacuous nature, they need an entire chapter of their own. Furthermore, the opening chapter on White Supremacy and Amerikanization should be understood as the groundwork that is laid for systemic racism. Now, with that being said, let's just say, for the sake of argument, that you have no unconscious biases or prejudices. Somehow, throughout your whole life, being subjected to the same social influences, popular sentiments, mass values, media agendas, and political propaganda as the rest of us, you've managed to stay cognizant, cautious, and skeptical of it all. None of the racist attitudes and beliefs held by the people who designed the Amerikan, and western society have developed in your psyche without first getting your acceptance and approval. And any of the ones you did actually develop were first subjected to a rigorous, objective, personal psychological screening process to determine its just, equal nature and moral superiority before you decided to consciously adopt it. Does this then exempt you from the ability to be racist? Unfortunately, no. It does not. As much as we want to believe that our character is enough to excuse us from being included in the system of oppression that is racism, white people do not have a choice. Because systemic racism does not require personal prejudice.

To reiterate, racism is more than just a bigoted attitude, derisive belief, or discriminatory bias. Although, racism does indeed stem from an attitude, belief, or prejudice, it also requires more to become racism. Otherwise, it just stays as a bigoted attitude, derisive belief, or discriminatory bias. What it requires is power. Kwame Ture (f.k.a. Stokely Carmichael) once said, "if a white man wants lynch me, that's his problem. If a white man has the power to lynch me, that's my problem". This is how systemic racism manifests. Having a prejudicial attitude towards people based solely on the color of their skin is racial bias or prejudice, not racism. Racism isn't about just a person's race and any related incidents that may occur as a result of being categorized as such. Racism is about how everyone of a particular race is affected as a whole on a daily basis. This is why our relationship to Black people and other people of color can be categorized as racism. This is how our attitudes and beliefs towards Black people and other people of color are racist on an individual level, but the reverse cannot also be true. Because when we express or demonstrate these attitudes and beliefs, we are expressing and demonstrating attitudes, beliefs and prejudices that are derived from, and a reflection of, the way in which our society, our politics, and our economy was built to function.

What we need to further understand is how our attitudes and beliefs have continued on far past a time when they were supported by the law. Just because laws change does not mean attitudes, beliefs, and prejudices change. Attitudes linger on far after laws have changed which are then handed down through family and social ties. The difference between laws and prejudices is that laws are much more flexible and open to interpretation than personal beliefs and prejudices. Our commitment to personal beliefs, attitudes, and prejudices supersedes our commitment to the law because we have a much deeper emotional investment in them. Therefore, as a result, we are able to find ways to circumvent or interpret the law in order to work with our attitudes and prejudices rather than adapting our attitudes and prejudices to fit within the law.

For example, during hiring practices, it was once legal for an employer to refuse employment to someone solely on the basis of being Black. However, while that specific reasoning is now illegal, it is still perfectly legal, as well as culturally acceptable, to refuse employment to someone based on other appearances. For instance, not until the year

2020 did the issue of dreadlocks as a natural Black hairstyle become contested as being professional enough for the workplace. Before then, it was considered to be reason enough to deny employment to someone with dreadlocks in their hair on the basis of so-called unprofessional appearance. Considering that Black hair naturally locks up as it grows, essentially, the message being conveyed is that Black people in their natural state are not qualified for specific jobs because their natural state does not fit the white definition of acceptable appearance, regardless of their competency level at performing the job; an aspect on which appearances have no effect. In other words, companies don't care how well Black people are at their job. If the company thinks they are too Black, then employment denial based on appearance supersedes employment acceptance based on ability.

Another example is the practice of "Redlining". Redlining was a common tactic used by mortgage lenders to keep Black people who were in the market for a house restricted to specific neighborhoods. Redlining is the practice of identifying certain neighborhoods as high credit risks. In the aftermath of the Great Depression, the U.S. government set out to evaluate the riskiness of mortgages, obviously as part of a preemptive effort to stave off another devastating dive in the stock market. In the late 1930s, the Home Owners' Loan Corporation "graded" neighborhoods into four categories, based in large part on their racial makeup. Neighborhoods with minority occupants were marked in red — hence the term "redlining — and were considered high-risk for mortgage lenders. Subsequently, creditworthy loan applicants were denied loans simply because they currently lived in the neighborhoods with the redlines around them. However, while the traditional practice of redlining has since been outlawed, mortgage lenders have found new ways to conduct redlining which would ensure the same outcome as traditional redlining. Between 2004 and 2008, Wells Fargo discriminated by steering approximately 4,000 African American and Hispanic wholesale borrowers into subprime mortgages when non-Hispanic white borrowers with similar credit profiles received prime loans. All the borrowers who were allegedly discriminated against were qualified for Wells Fargo mortgage loans according to Well Fargo's own underwriting criteria. Also, between 2004 and 2009, Wells Fargo discriminated by charging approximately 30,000 African American and Hispanic wholesale borrowers higher fees and rates than non-Hispanic white borrowers because of their race or national origin rather than the borrowers' credit worthiness or other objective criteria related to borrower risk. These discriminatory lending practices were a major contributing factor to the high mortgage default rates in poorer neighborhoods when the housing bubble burst. You would think that the lawsuit Wells Fargo faced by the Federal Justice Department for these despicable shows of obvious racism would be enough to prevent these racist neo-redlining practices from continuing. However, in 2019 Wells Fargo again came under fire by settling a lawsuit from 2017 with the city of Philadelphia for the exact same racial discrimination practices. And it doesn't stop there. In 2021, Freddie Mac issued a report on a study they conducted between January 1, 2015, and December 31, 2020. This report explicitly outlines the value disparities by appraisers in Black and Latinx neighborhoods compared to those of white neighborhoods. Freddie Mac found out that appraisals in the communities more than 80 percent Black were lower than the contract price 13.3 percent of the time, compared to 7.4 percent in white communities. The study also showed that it's not just a few appraisers who are perpetuating this gap. The study states clearly that, "These results suggest that a large portion of appraisers who performed enough appraisals in both Black and White tracts exhibit statistically significant Black versus White gaps,". What this means is that when appraisals fall below the contracted sale price, "families might miss out on the full wealth-building benefits of homeownership or may be unable to get the financing needed to achieve the American Dream in the first place." Between denying loans on prejudice grounds, racial covenants written into deeds, and significantly shorting Black and Brown people on the value of their homes, redlining is being conducted in one fashion or another. Because laws are more flexible than beliefs.

The relationship between laws and society is politics at an everyday level. We tend to think of politics as being limited to what happens in Washington D.C. or down at city hall. To the common person, politics is practiced in a professional arena by the people we vote for to do so. We think voting for politicians to represent us and make our decisions for us is where our political involvement stops. I mean, after all, that's what these people get paid to do, right? Well, be that as it may, it by no means exempts us from political engagement, nor can or should it. Considering that the relationship between laws and society is what politics looks like at an everyday level, then the fact that we the people are who make up society and, as society, we are precisely who are affected by the laws that are made, then, by reason, we cannot escape waking up every single day and making decisions in our personal lives that have political repercussions. The personal is political and the political is personal.

Additionally, socially speaking, racism intersects with classism at the crossroads of exploitation, mass incarceration, and degradation. It is with the power of degradation that comes along with classism that we are able to attach certain social stigmas to people who experience poverty as a result of racism. This degradation counteracts any struggles for progress that Black people have made. Let me clarify what I mean through example. In every single other developed country in the world, public transportation is a social norm. Access to, use, and the efficiency of public transportation is the standard and preferred means of travel for every so-called first world country. Even those who own cars regularly use public transportation and reserve their cars for either weekend or holiday travel. Busses, subways, and els are more common, more frequent, and reach more places than those of the U.S. Anyone who takes public transportation is considered to be just following social standards with no regard, second thought, or unconscious bias towards what their social status may be. In the U.S. however, it's quite a different story. In the U.S., ownership and regular use of one's own private transportation is considered to be a sign of status, independence, and financial security. Amerikans have a social stigma that is embedded within our psyches which tells us that anyone without their own car must be poor, struggling, second class citizens undeserving of basic human respect and dignity. Especially in smaller metro areas, public transportation is considered a sign of hardship. Of course, thanks to Ronald Reagan's illustration of the "welfare queen", these prejudices have the tendency to be laced with racism. We paint these preconceived images of them in our heads; often times without even intending to. A single Black woman on the bus with children gets pre-judged as promiscuous, jobless, mooching off the system, with multiple baby daddies. Single Black men on the bus are pre-judged as broke, jobless, deadbeat, and lazy. The details of these prejudices vary depending on the person or people they're aimed at but, the fundamental aspect of race as the basis for inferiorizing them through a class lens remains the same.

However, even in the U.S., it hasn't always been this way. At one time, taking the bus or the streetcar was a perfectly respectable thing to do, by both white and Black people alike. Throngs of people flocked to and from their jobs using public transit without a second thought. So how did taking the bus become such a stigmatized source of ridicule in the U.S.? It's a combination of what's known as "white flight" mixed with backlash for the civil rights movement.

Essentially, white flight is what created the suburbs. The urban areas that we now often implicitly associate with Black people and culture were once predominantly, most even exclusively, white neighborhoods. How-ever, after the onset of integration and the gradual taboo of Jim Crow era policies, Black people began migrating from rural areas into the cities where all the good, higher paying production and manufacturing jobs were. Because these jobs were once exclusively held by white people, naturally their surrounding areas were also predominantly white. Since Black people were now considered by law to be qualified for these jobs, naturally they began to relocate in order to be closer to their work. The attitudes of white people, of course, prevailed, and as Black people began to populate the urban areas, the white people who once resided in those neighborhoods began their great migration outwards to the suburbs.

The economic arrangement then began to follow suit. As white peo-ple started moving outwards, away from the inner cities, so too did the money. Even to this day in 2021, Black men earn $0.13 less than white men for the exact same job. That number was much higher in the 1950's and 60's. And Black women earn the least amount of money of anyone in the U.S. So, since white people have always made more money for the same jobs as their Black counterparts, naturally, more and more white people began to purchase automobiles in order to shorten the commute time that had been greatly extended due to the increased distance be-tween home in the suburbs and work in the cities. The sudden rise in auto ownership among white suburban residents was, in fact, even under-scored by the auto industry who, after suffering a number of lawsuits and anti-car campaigns from the families and communities of injured or killed pedestrians only a few decades before, had lobbied to make the streets that were once used more for walking than for driving on, exclusive to the use of automobiles. This then led to the whole of the U.S.'s infrastructure being built around the assumption that automobiles were the default means of transportation. The auto industry's monopolization of roads, the building of towns and suburbs around the assumption of auto own-ership, and the wage gap between white and Black workers created the perfect conditions for white flight, which subsequently greatly reduced the demand for busses in suburban areas. As busses ran less and less out to the suburbs but remained running in the inner cities, the overall de-mographic of ridership inevitably changed to match the new formation of segregation. This left the perfect opportunity for white people to retaliate against Black people for the bus boycotts that launched the civil rights movement into a worthy challenge against Jim Crow. It was now the op-timal time to start demonizing and alienating the people who rode the bus.

With automobile ownership on a steady rise, complimented by a sharp, not-so-coincidental spike in the 1950's, and a recent legal win for Black people's right to sit wherever they like, public transportation became less and less appealing and practical to white people. This was the beginning of vehicle ownership as a status symbol. The so-called Amerikan dream is personified by the Amerikan middle class. Setting the bar for what constitutes success in society, white ownership of vehicles was now included among the other symbols of desired status that conveyed the impression of success and comfort. Along with individual, private living quarters, gainful steady employment, regular meals, television sets, backyard swimming pools, and yearly family vacations, leaving only the question of how far up one has managed to climb their status symbolized in part by the type of vehicle they owned, the Amerikan dream, and all the material possessions that signified it, was set by white people who couldn't stand to live in the same neighborhood as Black people.

Taking the bus didn't become stigmatized as a sign of low class, poverty, and all the racial prejudices that come with it until white people moved out to the suburbs and stopped taking it to work. Now it is widely considered to be an indicator for one's personal station in life. However, because public transportation became a sign of poverty and shame, it then began to operate as such. Concerning the issue of public transportation, the cause and the effect have become the same. Because the busses became associated with poor people and Black people have systematically been held in poverty, we then subconsciously assume every negative racial stereotype about Black people that intersects with the stereotypes of poor people to be true whenever we see them using public transportation.

However, the same cannot be said for white people who use public transportation. The automatic stigmas that are attached to Black people who take the bus are not automatically attached to white people. The simple appearance of a white person on the bus does not conjure the same thoughts and prejudices in our heads. Seeing a white man in khaki shorts or a white woman in yoga pants on the bus evokes the assumption of an exception. We tend to reconcile their appearance on the bus as either some kind of deviation from their everyday life or a presumption that they take it for convenience rather than necessity. The average, everyday white person using public transportation is automatically assumed to be using it as supplementary transportation. In order for us to attach any negative prejudices to white people on public transportation, both the circumstances as well as the personal appearance of the individuals themselves have to be extreme and obvious for any prejudice or stigma to be assigned to them on the bus. Their behavior has to be erratic, unpredictable, and out of the ordinary. Their clothes and personal hygiene have to be shabby, unkempt, and off-putting. Only then do we assume the use of public transportation to be included in their personal indicators of poverty. And only then do we attach negative biases and stigmas to them.

The stigma of public transportation is racist because it, like all racist beliefs, is backed by power. Social stigmas are backed by the power of assignment. Every single social stigma in the modern western world that has any power to affect the lives of other people has been developed and applied by white people. The ability to do this stems from the power differential that white people have in society over all others. Even those stigmas assigned to other, lower class white people were done so by the upper classes of rich white people. Holding the majority of the world's wealth affords all white people - even those who do not personally hold the wealth, but simply because they have the same skin color as those who do - the ability to determine social stigmas and apply them according to their own beliefs. This, again, finds us at the crossroads of racism and classism. The racist notions that are evoked, yet often unrealized when we see these otherwise ineffectual, everyday events are part of, and caused by, a larger picture. What we as white people need to realize is two specific things. The first is that these prejudices aren't necessarily conscious thoughts that we intentionally choose to have. They're conjured up as subconscious assumptions that are produced by the conditioning we've received over the years. This conditioning is a result of social stigmas and prejudices that penetrated the psyche of society long before we were born. Because these prejudices and attitudes developed and took hold of society at large long before our time, we experience these thoughts on a more visceral and fleeting level. They're often very short lived and can even occur in the form of a feeling rather than a conscious thought. However, they can have a profoundly damaging affect if we fail to recognize and correct them in ourselves and each other.

Secondly, every example and argument previously mentioned all have one thing in common. They're all supported by power. These aren't simple cases of individual prejudice or discrimination. These issues occurred and continue to occur on a scale that can only be used to measure an entire community's relationship to society, politics, and economy. Our racist attitudes and prejudices can only be labeled and considered racist because they're backed by the power of discriminatory hiring practices, they're reinforced by the power of a concerted effort by banks to keep Black people contained within specific neighborhoods, they're supported by social stigmas assigned by white people on the use of public transportation by Black people and other people of color. White heroism is backed by the power of imperialism. Cultural appropriation is backed by the power to determine pop culture and mainstream media. Police and prisons are backed by the profitability of keeping crime rates high and prisons filled. Language is backed by the power of education and imperialism. Fetishism is backed by the power to control entertainment. And so on, and so on. Yet, all of these forms and manifestations of racism are rooted in the greed for money and dominance either through labor or consumption.

What all of this illustrates is the development of society over time given specific circumstances and conditions. The influence that law has on popular opinion and prejudices; the unrequested, yet still received, benefits that we are afforded just for being white when people in positions of power enact their prejudices and attitudes; the unconscious biases that we don't choose to develop; the social stigmas that we are all subject to adopting yet personally cannot dissolve from society; the automatic presumption that illegality is synonymous with evil; and the separation of self from the rest of our community in search of personal enrichment and any cost all combine together to create the conditions that develop a society wherein certain people are automatically favored at the expense of others. The key word here is "automatic". When a society is built, the people who build it have to choose social, political, and economic functions to implement in order for society to run. The ones that our ancestors chose were implemented with racism because they themselves believed in their own superiority. Therefore, when racism is built into the social, political and economic functions of society, said society will operate accordingly. Inevitably, the ways in which the racism within these societal functions is applied will morph over time. However, because it is a part of the system's operation, it will not disappear. What it will do is begin to operate under its own momentum. Therein lies the automation of racism in society today. The social, political, and economic functions that were started by our European ancestors are the foundations of Amerikan and Western society and have been so even though they are no longer here to perpetuate them. Because that's how the functions of society work. They only need to be implemented or adopted by society. They do not need constant oversight or continuous, manual operation in order to perpetually function. Ergo, because our society today operates on the same foundations as were accepted and implemented yesterday, we as white people still hold the same favored position in society today as our ancestors did yesterday. Because this favoritism is now automatic, so too is the persecution that it causes. Neither this favoritism nor the corresponding persecution are necessarily a conscious choice by all of us but rather, they are the consequences of the choices our ancestors made centuries ago when they decided to arrange society the way they did. Nevertheless, most of us are very unaware of how history developed and what course it took for us to get here.

Racism does not just look like one person hurling racial slurs at another person. If human beings could stay completely devoid of prejudices and biases, then society would naturally develop justly and equitably. However, that's not the way we developed over time. Whether it's possible for humans to ever be completely devoid of prejudice is a sociological argument up for debate, one that we won't get into. What I'm sure we all can agree on, however, is that within our current society, right now, the way it is today, all humans will develop some kind of prejudice or bias about one thing or another. And that's where it starts. Racism begins with the belief that people's physical differences make up different races. Racism then proceeds under the assumption that one race is superior to all others. From there, it builds an entire society on these beliefs and assumptions. Racism is a particular way in which society functions where one race of people who are thought to be superior to all others are favored through the persecution of all those who are not of the so-called superior race. Thus, the everyday lives of anyone who is not socially recognized as the favored race are negatively impacted in ways that can be hard to recognize if we ourselves are not subjected to them. This favoritism manifests solely due to the assumption that those who are favored are superior to those who are not. When we see racism play out on an individual scale, it is because these individual instances are symptomatic of the way society is built and operates.

The functions of said society are both economic and political but, tend to occur most evidently, although not exclusively, on a social scale. Along with the way we're taught about it in school, this too is why so many of us have such a strong misunderstanding of racism. Most of us take the current state of the world for granted. But our modern reality is not a given. It was not inevitable for us to end up here. The state of the world today did not have to happen. Nevertheless, due to our lack of understanding history, the course that it took to get to today, and the stops it made along the way, we are often only able to recognize racism in a social context in individual instances and have a difficult time placing it in the context of a bigger picture. The reason so many people deny the existence of racism is because they are either unable or choose not to see the way society has developed over time to create the conditions under which racism is able to persist so effortlessly today. They often look at the laws and economy the way they exist today and take them for granted. We assume that the way our world exists today is the way that it was supposed to happen. Most of us do not examine the development of laws and economics over the course of time to see how their negative impacts in the past continue to have resounding affects today. Nor do we take the time to analyze the laws in relation to an alternative way of organizing a society.

For instance, when we think about crime, our automatic assumption is that a rise in crime means we need more police. Rarely, however, is this automatic assumption thought through. It's easy to cling to an answer that is more readily available and easier to conceptualize. But that doesn't make it useful or effective. When we see a spike in crime and violence, imagining more police on the streets is realistic to us. It's an idea that's relatively simple to grasp. Unfortunately, that's usually where it stops. We don't ever seem to consider what the implications of more police are. Nor do we seem to ever consider any other factors involved. Answering a rise in crime with an automatic social response of more police is too far removed from the context within which crime occurs. If we compare neighborhoods with high crime rates to neighborhoods with low crime rates, we see that the presence of police is lower in places with lower crimes rates. That alone is enough to tell us that more police is not the answer. However, that is not the only difference. The conditions of these neighborhoods compared to each other is also glaringly obvious. Poverty runs rampant in neighborhoods with higher crime rates. Homelessness is higher. The availability and quality of health care is worse. The accessibility to nutrition is worse. The quality of education is worse. The pay for jobs is worse. The condition of housing is worse. The list goes on. Furthermore, it's not exactly a coincidence that many racists assume the word "ghetto" is synonymous with Black neighborhoods. This is because Black people have systematically been kept in a state of poverty and poverty is how ghettos are created. Just ask the Jewish people in the ghettos of 1939 Poland. If poverty is the most obvious where crime is the most likely, then the people who are experiencing the poverty are the ones who will have to endure the intensity of our answer to that crime. This is because crime doesn't begin as a personal moral failure. Despite what the movies tell you, people don't just decide to become evil. To assume that some people are destined to be the villain and that breaking the law is what makes someone a villain is over simplified and plays right into the hands of racist mentalities. On the contrary, all crime starts out as a survival mechanism for poverty. From there, crime and street life build an organic culture of its own that ends up attracting younger people to it. But crime doesn't start out that way. If crime started out as a means of survival rather than a culture or a mentality, then changing and regulating that culture or mentality cannot end it. Only eliminating poverty can do that.

Answering a rise in crime with a force that has proven itself over time to be ineffective in lowering crime can only mean one of two things. Either those who make the decisions on how to deal with crime have not thought this answer all the way through or they are okay with the existence of what police have proven themselves to be effective at. Violence, abuse, brutality, suppression, murder, and enslavement are the only things cops have been able to accomplish since they were first instituted. The presence of police does not endorse personal responsibility. It endorses abuse. And it does this through fear. However, these responses are conditioned within us because of how prevalent they are in society. These responses become automatic and prevalent because they are normalized. We've been subjected to these ideas and their occurrences for so long and so often that they become reasonable, everyday expectations. If the idea of restorative justice and community self-defense were just as normalized to us, then the idea of police and prisons would be just as abstract and unrealistic. And this is how racist ideas become systematized racism.

Popular attitudes and prejudices eventually take hold in certain pockets of society. Most often these are the parts of society where the most power is held because these attitudes and beliefs correlate with power. Supremacist attitudes and beliefs will appeal the most to people who have more power than others. So when these popular attitudes and prejudices are adopted by people with both financial and political power such as bankers, CEOs, business owners, captains of industry, mass media owners, politicians, lobbyists, and all the rest of those with the political and economic control of the world, they become implemented politically and economically under corporate bylaws of operation, media opinions pushed as factual reporting, appealing to people's sense of patriotism and unquestioning loyalty, social behaviors that become normalized in our everyday life, and even things that we find humorous and entertaining. All these areas of life are conditioned by ideas that have become normal and acceptable in society. Thus, the implementation of these attitudes and beliefs in politics and economics inevitably affect the way society is organized, the way it functions, and our relationship with it on a daily basis.

Since the construction and operation of society is affected by an unequal distribution of power and this unequal distribution of power is based on beliefs and attitudes that are prejudice towards people of a particular race or races, then those of us who are of the same race as the ones with the power are automatically afforded certain privileges in society. Often times, however, we have difficulty seeing these privileges because we're so separated from those who are excluded from them. These benefits are even further obscured because we didn't ask for them. We never asked the judges and police to give us the benefit of the doubt, more patience, more leniency, and less violence than others. We didn't request that banks approve us for home loans simply based on our skin color or zip code. We were not the ones who wrote racial covenants into contracts for deed. We never expected to receive better textbooks, higher paid and more attentive teachers, smaller class sizes, better food for lunches, and less police in our schools. We didn't ask for doctors to be more caring, compassionate, and spend more time trying to help us when we go to the clinic than they do in other neighborhoods. We didn't double check to make sure we get paid more than Black, Brown, and Native people for doing the same job as them. We've had to work our whole lives too. We weren't exactly born with a silver spoon in our mouths either. So, seeing that we are given benefits that we didn't ask for can be difficult. Especially when we feel like the assertion that we have these privileges is an attack on all the hard work we've done and all the struggles we've overcome. But that's the point. We're afforded these extra benefits because the system automatically gives them to us just because of the way we look. We need to accept that having certain benefits and privileges in society doesn't invalidate all our hard work and struggle. No one is saying that. What is being said is that our hard work and struggle were not a result of the color of our skin. It is the color of our skin that made our struggles in life less difficult than they would have been; less difficult than others.

Let's remember to keep in mind that none of this suggests that all white people have the same amount of power. We do not have the power to go around directly lynching Black people with impunity. Well... not anymore anyway. We do not own slaves nor do most of us come from money that was accrued by enslavement. We do not control the hiring practices of major corporations or the lending standards of banks. We have no power over police, judges, or prosecutors. We cannot snap our fingers and instantly change the quality of housing or education in any given part of the world. None of this is meant to imply that every white person in society had a hand in creating the social, economic, and political system that operates so unequally and unjustly. That is not the argument. What is the argument is that there was a time not too long ago when we did, in fact, have that power to lynch Black people at will. Just because we were treated worse than the rich white people, the common white man was still, in fact, treated better than the enslaved Black people. This part of Amerikan history is undeniable. Everyone is aware of the Atlantic slave trade, chattel slavery and the gruesome, barbaric, sadistic, inhumane, back-breaking conditions imposed upon Black people for 300 years. We're all taught about the Jim Crow south that cropped up after the Civil War and lasted for about another 75 years. The existence of lynch mobs and race rioters, sundown towns, the prominent terrorism of the KKK, the spectacle of public humiliation, the excessive use of force and brutality by police, abuse of authority by bosses, and the egregious conditions that were forced upon Black people through the so-called "separate but equal" laws (just to name a few of the inequalities and injustices) are no secret to anyone. Well, the system that imposed all of this on Black people which, by default, was a benefit to us simply because we're white, is still in place to this day. Which means that even though we don't have the power to privately own enslaved people or go around personally lynching Black people unless we have a police uniform on, much of the privileges that came as byproducts from once being granted that power are still being afforded to us to this day. Similarly, many of the restrictions, disadvantages, and injustices that came along with the threat of being lynched at any given time are also still in place to this day. We are still seen as more innocent and less dangerous than Black people. We are seen by society to be more trustworthy, harder working, more educated, and better behaved. We're given more compassion and understanding for our addictions. Doctors are far more likely to believe us about our pain. And we are more likely to be hired by a company despite our appearances or background checks.

Neither does all this suggest that we created the concepts and institutions used to develop racism. We didn't create prejudice, discrimination, or biases based on skin color. Nor did we invent slavery. These are concepts and institutions that have been around for a majority of human existence. What we did do was adopt the two, combine them, and added in our own unprecedented levels of brutality, inhumanity, barbarism, degradation, and violence. We implemented and maintained this system of racialized slavery using the aforementioned violence to amass obscene fortunes. Then, once we were done with it, we thought it would be good enough to just do away with the private ownership of slaves without also discarding the society that was produced by slavery. The U.S. is the system that slavery built. Slavery that used race as it's determining factor, greed as it's motivating force, and every type of violence imaginable as it's means of maintain a perpetual existence.

What all this comes down to is how we're involved in the way racism operates. First, the reason our personal attitudes and beliefs are discussed throughout the book is because that's what develops out of the previous attitudes and beliefs that our ancestors held. It was with their prejudice attitudes and beliefs that our ancestors created society. As such, the ones that we exhibit today grew out of the ones that our ancestors exhibited and built society with yesterday. Ridding ourselves and each other of these personal prejudices and biases is part and parcel to eliminating white supremacy. Second, simply being born white does not make us racist. However, being born white into a society that affords us benefits and privileges at the expense of others simply because we are white does indeed make us racist. White Supremacy and racism are the same thing. If we are born white into a white supremacist society then, by default, we are automatically treated by that society as superior to all others. Therefore, while our participation in white supremacy may be involuntary, our participation in society is required. We cannot function in life being separated from society. As Aristotle once pointed out, there is no such thing as the pre-social human condition. Humans are social creatures and as such, have always operated within a society of one form or another. Being born into a white supremacist society forces us as white people to be complicit in a social dynamic that most of us would never choose to be a part of if ever given the choice. This dynamic dictates that we live our lives according to the way this society functions. If the functions of this society persecute others and benefit us, then we have no other choice but to be a part of the racism on which society operates. As white people in a white supremacist society, we are automatic beneficiaries of an unequal society. Receiving these benefits and privileges that we do not ask for means that no matter what our personal attitudes and beliefs are, we are still apart of racism and, as such, still racist until that social dynamic no longer exists.

Chapter 16
Ignorance

Maya Angelou said "You do the best you can with what you know. Then, when you know better, you do better." But let's be real, some of us would rather remain ignorant than do better. Ignorance is the state of lacking knowledge or information. When we lack knowledge, by default, we are not being our best selves. Not being our best selves, for any reason, has a negative impact on many other people besides ourselves. In order to have a more positive impact on the world, we have to be willing to rid ourselves of our ignorance.

Ignorance can come in two basic forms: willful or unintentional. Unintentional ignorance is found in people with little knowledge and understanding of the issues facing modern society as well as the dynamic relationships with which society operates on a day-to-day basis. Although not necessarily through lack of want, the unintentionally ignorant person just doesn't know that the world is much different than what they were taught to believe. Through circumstances generally beyond their own control, the unintentionally ignorant person simply just did not have the opportunity to meet life on any other terms other than what was accessible to them. In other words, because their lives took a certain course, unintentionally ignorant people did not know that there was more information out there than what was made available to them. Unintentional ignorance is often recognized in one of two ways. Either by opinions and world views based on information that has since been debunked and outdated. Or by sheer lack of knowledge on a particular topic at all. There can be a particular innocence to unintentional ignorance that, in some cases, may help to mitigate any damage that asserting ignorant views is likely to have. However, that's only if they are willing to accept correction and do better with the new information they are given.

Willful ignorance, on the other hand, is much more sinister. Willful ignorance is the conscious choice to retain beliefs and attitudes even in light of new information. This new information is generally the type that refutes, disproves, or overtakes the information that is the basis for our attitudes, biases, and prejudices. The willfully ignorant person purposely hangs on to their worldview despite being provided with new information or alternative perspectives that offer a better understanding on a given topic. Hanging onto this attitude or worldview stems from fear of a change in their relationship with society and reality. Most often, this worldview has not changed much throughout the course of their life and is more than likely similar to how they related to the world as a child or young adult. Willful ignorance is also usually accompanied by arrogance or a false humility that comes across as more dismissive than humble. The irony of being arrogant in our own ignorance would be laughable if it wasn't so dangerous. In either instance, however, rather than attempting to further understand this new information or alternative perspective, the urge to stay ignorant takes hold and instead, the desire for comfort becomes the most important goal. This because the new information holds the potential to completely change how we see the world and subsequently, how we relate to it. This, ultimately, is the bottom line. Our current understanding of the world is comfortable to us. We've built our entire reality on it. All of the paradoxes have been reconciled. Any further contradictions to this understanding threaten our comfort. And remaining comfortable in our everyday lives is the driving force behind willful ignorance.

This commitment to misunderstanding has bred some of the most ridiculous and migraine headache inducing arguments that are used by white people to justify or deny their racism. The cognitive dissonance, mental gymnastics, and utter disregard for thinking their arguments through leave these arguments wide open for scrutiny and humiliation. These arguments are almost never rooted in fact but, instead they follow a logic that preys on white emotion and ego. These arguments and attitudes are contrived solely to make us feel superior, infallible, and absolved of responsibility. The logic holds up only as far as it allows us to reserve the right to judge others while simultaneously allowing us to shed the guilt for our prejudice. Because that's what is comfortable to us. Feeling judged for a legacy that favors us based simply on our skin color is a fear that plagues white society to the bone. And the only way we have to escape that judgement is by feeling like we instead have the right to judge. So, we develop arguments that at first seem to make sense yet, given any amount of in depth thought or criticism, fail miserably to stand up to reason. Beyond allowing white people to feel a sense of equal oppression with Black people and other people of color, which gives us a sense of entitlement to judge others, the breakdown of the logic that holds these arguments together is almost instantaneous. Exploring some of these arguments and attitudes will illuminate just how asinine, unreasonable, and therefore racist, these arguments and attitudes are.

Police killings

As of 2020 there are over 230 million white people living in the U.S. Compared to that, there are also about 42 million Black people living in the U.S. If we break that down into numbers that are easier to comprehend, we could say that there are 230 white people and 42 Black people. If police kill 50 white people a year and 20 Black people a year, who gets killed at a much higher rate? Black people. Because 20 is about .48% of 42 while 50 is only about .22% of 230. Translated back into realistic numbers, we see that 200 is a higher percentage of 42 million than 500 is of 230 million. So, while it may be true that more white people are being killed per year by police than Black people, Black people are getting killed at a much higher rate. Despite how morbidly sickening this realization is, the reality stands that Black people getting killed at a higher rate means that if police don't stop murdering Black people, then they face extinction faster than white people. They would be wiped out simply because their skin is Black. At that point, it doesn't matter how you define racism, that fact fits the description.

Yet and still, the underlying issue here is how problematic police in Amerika are. Using the argument that more white people are killed per year by police than Black people still highlights just how dangerous and destructive police are to our communities. This means that there is a shared, mutual interest in addressing the problem of police in Amerika. If you are not addressing the problem along with and on the side of Black people, then the only reason you even cite the stats in the first place is as a way to try and prove Black people wrong about their own experiences and oppression. You don't actually care that the police are murdering people with impunity, you just can't be bothered to accept the reality of racism. Because nothing makes white people more uncomfortable and agitated than when Black people try to assert their humanity.

Speech Patterns: the "Blaccent"

We all have speech patterns. Different ways of speaking that are unique to each one of us. When developed over time, these patterns eventually become our own. However, although our speech patterns are exclusive to ourselves, there are multiple factors involved that influence the development of those patterns. The two major contributing factors to the development of speech patterns are our parents or guardians as well as our immediate environment.

The biggest influence on our speech patterns is our parents or the people that raise us. Our mom is the first person we hear speak. The person or people that raise us is usually who we hear speak the most throughout our childhood. They make impressions on us when we're young that will last us for the rest of our lives. Furthermore, it's important to understand that our parents' or guardian's speech patterns were developed by their parents or guardians as well as their environment also. Our speech patterns aren't just developed over the course of our own lives. They're also a product of our ancestors' speech pattern development.

The second biggest influence on our speech patterns is our environment. The people we are around on a daily basis, particularly when we're kids and young adults. Yes, people like friends, acquaintances, neighbors, teachers, older siblings, etc. But also, the neighborhoods and communities that we live in. All of these things combine together to influence the way our speech patterns develop.

What this means is that the very distinct speech patterns of Black people, particularly in Amerika, result from the conditions and situations that they exclusively were subjected to. Black people, and Black people alone, had a very specific set of historical experiences that impacted the way their speech developed. The reason you can usually tell if a person is Black over the phone started way, way before you or they were even born. When their ancestors were kidnapped from the shores of Africa, they didn't speak English. They were forced to learn English as a condition of their enslavement. Naturally, being from a foreign land, as with anyone who doesn't speak English as a Native language, the development of their

English came with an accent. From that point, their children heard them speaking English and developed it as their native language. However, the children heard their parents speaking English with an accent much different than the white kids who they were playing with or the overseers who were constantly berating them and their parents. Due to these conditions, Black people developed speech patterns that were impacted by two or more very different dialects of English. After further being confined to their own neighborhoods in one way or another, their speech patterns were reinforced generation after generation. They then began to culturally evolve with their own forms of the English vernacular which, again, greatly influenced their speech patterns.

So no, growing up around Black people is not enough to explain why you sound like that. Neither your parents nor your grandparents nor your ancestors were subjected to those conditions. If tens of thousands of Arabs and Asians can live and work in Black neighborhoods without developing the Blaccent then clearly that's not "just the way you talk". Every single word you say comes with a conscious pre-thought for how you can adjust your mouth, lips, and tongue in order for the word to come out making you sound more Black. You speak that way because you have an identity crisis. You have no culture and no idea who you are. You go around telling people to "cash me outside, hawbot dat" because you think that by aligning yourself with the most oppressed, marginalized community in Amerika, it'll validate your existence enough to hide your inability to create your own identity. You sound ignorant. Not because you sound Black. But because you sound white trying sound Black.

The "N" Word

Earlier in the book we touched on the infamous "N" word. Here we're going to review the history of this word as well as explore some white people's inexplicable urge to want to use it. However, before we dive into this topic, it's important to establish the direction this section intends to go. There's a very stark difference between those white people who use the "N" word to purposely degrade and separate themselves from Black people because they feel superior to them, and those white people who use the "N" word because they think they have access to and are a complimentary part of the Black community. While both of these mindsets are ignorant, those of us who think we have the right to use it because we have Black friends or a Black partner or have been told we can by Black people are the ones who seem to be in the most need of understanding. Those white people who use the "N" word in a derogatory sense pretty much know how and why they are using it. That ignorance that cannot be changed by anyone but themselves and I have no interest in trying to convince someone who is intent on being racist why they shouldn't be racist. However, those of us who use the "N" word as a way to align ourselves with the Black community generally don't understand why it's racist for us to do so. For the most part, we believe that because we don't have a conscious desire to actually be racist or that we've been invited to use it by close friends, that we are absolved of the racism that is otherwise entrenched in the word. Nothing could be further from the truth.

The question is, why would you even want to say it? Why do you want to say it so bad? Especially given our history with the word. When our ancestors first incorporated the "N" word into the English language, it was an intentional way for us to remind Black people that they were socially and - in our opinion, biologically - inferior to us. This word became a comprehensive way for us to dehumanize, inferiorize, and keep Black people psychologically subordinate to us. Centuries of brutality, torture, rape, enslavement, poverty and lynching are now summed up with one word that white people can and often do resort to whenever we feel that our sense of superiority is threatened.

Not ones to succumb so easily to circumstance or psychological warfare, Black people took the word from white people and began using it amongst themselves. Essentially, the appropriation of this word by Black people robbed the word of its oppressive power. That's not to say that it is no longer offensive when we use it. However, the word no longer has the psychological effect of degradation that it once had. Now, when Black people use that word amongst themselves, it is either a term of endearment or a benign reference. The power that was once contained within that word has changed. When used among Black people, at most, the "N" word is an implied acknowledgment of all the pain and suffering that each other's ancestors have been through. At least it is an ineffectual colloquialism that has costed them hundreds of trillions of dollars, tens of millions of lives, hundreds of years, and countless drops of blood, sweat, and tears. It no longer belongs to white people. If, for any reason, white people use the "N", it reverts right back to its original intent. This is because of our historical relationship to the word. Our relationship with the "N" word has never been one that allows us to use it in any other kind of context other than to dehumanize and try to impose a sense of power over Black people. Even if that's not what we intend to do, by using the "N" word, our historical relationship to it automatically attaches a derogatory and dehumanizing connotation to it.

In fact, those of us who attempt to substitute filler words for it are no better. Inserting words like "ninja", "nicki", or any other phonetically similar word in conversational places where a Black person may use the actual "N" word is just as ignorant as if you had used the actual word itself. Everyone knows what you mean. And everyone knows what you want to say. You're just too scared that you'll get punched in the face for saying it. But you're not any less ignorant for not actually saying the word.

Given our long and shameful history with the "N" word, we are no longer allowed to use it without consequences. No matter what the reason is, the "N" word is not ours to use. It belongs to Black people now. They paid for it; it's theirs. If you know the words to a song well enough to sing along to it, then you know them well enough to refrain from saying that word while you're singing along. Attempting to use it because we feel like we have special, VIP access to the Black community is ignorant. Until white people have a similar long, brutal, bloody, oppressive, history that leads to modern day social and economic disenfranchisement with political marginalization that was all brought on by Black people's greed and superiority complex, it is unacceptable for white people to use the "N" word in any context or for any reason.

The Confederate Flag

The highly contested issue of the Confederate flag and some people's desire to display it proudly is really very simple. Many of us who have this repugnant urge to exhibit the Confederate Flag like it's some sort of family crest or coat of arms will go to the farthest reaches of the galaxy to come back with the most asinine justifications in order to avoid being labeled a racist while still honoring their proud symbol of the south. Because racists really want to be racist without being seen as a racist. So, let's just clarify that yes, it was about state's rights. The right for states to maintain slavery. Yes, it was about rebellion against the establishment. Rebellion against an establishment that was pushing to abolish slavery. Yes, it is about heritage. A heritage of slavery, oppression, and genocide. If it's a matter of wanting to fly it because your great-grandfather fought and died under it, then it's probably in your best interest to accept that he fought and died for slavery. If that's what makes you proud to be a southerner, then you are definitely a true patriot.

Please try to understand that the evidence far surpasses the rhetoric and your personal feelings on the matter are not enough disprove 180 years of data. The articles of secession mention slavery over 80 times. The only real difference between the original U.S. Constitution and the Confederate Constitution is, in fact, the explicit continuation of slavery and its so-called benefit to Black people. One article banned any Confederate state from making slavery illegal and required that any new state acquired by the Confederacy allow slavery. 4 out of the 11 Confederate states explicitly wrote chattel slavery to be the reason for their secession into their declaration. The vice president of the Confederate States Alexander Hamilton Stephens gave a speech saying that: "The new Constitution has put at rest forever all the agitating questions relating to our peculiar institutions--African slavery as it exists among us--the proper status of the negro in our form of civilization... Our new Government is founded upon exactly the opposite ideas; its foundations are laid, its cornerstone rests, upon the great truth that the negro is not equal to the white man; that slavery, subordination to the superior race, is his natural and normal condition."

Any excuse to display the Confederate flag is a feeble one. No matter how far removed from white supremacy your reasoning may be, whatever personal attachment you have to the Confederate flag is rooted I racism. If you're proud to be a southerner, then fine. If you feel like you want to convey that to the world, then by all means, go ahead and do so. A dirty John Deere hat or worn-out cowboy hat will serve that purpose just as effectively. So will driving an unnecessarily big truck with even bigger tires while wearing a giant belt buckle shaped like Texas. There are plenty of other symbols available to display your southern pride that aren't rooted in the subjugation, brutality, and enslavement of Black people. However, using blatant and intentional symbols of white supremacy to proclaim your southern pride is either intentional ignorance or intentional racism. It is virtually impossible to live in the 21st century and not know what the Confederate flag represents. And trying to revise historically proven facts in order to justify your displays of racism without being considered racist is not only ignorance, but also a denial of reality. Because at the end of the day, it doesn't matter what the flag means to you. What matters is the people that endured hundreds of years of terror, brutality, enslavement, and the most disgusting, inhuman treatment of one people by another through an institution that flag fought to maintain only to see their descendants have to be subjected to that trauma all over again just because you have some unhealthy attachment to a piece of cloth that represents the very ignorance you exhibit by flying it.

The Irish

The tumultuous history between England and Ireland goes back hundreds of years. Between the Catholic church and the Protestant rebellion, Ireland has been seeped in conflict with the Brits. It reached its boiling point when young upstart Oliver Cromwell decided that Ireland was ripe for colonization and therefore, the Irish people were inferior to all other whites. This attitude was then carried over by the British colonists that later invaded the Amerikas. It also laid the groundwork for indentured servitude.

Since the onset of capitalism by Europeans in the 16th century, white people have been in the market for free or cheap forced labor (ironically, all while pushing the notion of hard work as the virtuous path to success). Since the British attitude towards Irish people was only slightly better than their attitude towards Black people and all people of color, they, of course, found it perfectly acceptable to impose their military and economic power over the Irish in order to extort cheap labor from them. During a time when Irish were not even considered to be included in the same category as other white people, many wealthy businessmen and farming colonists took advantage of people who they would later consider to be their own. While most of the southern wealthy elite were busy ushering in and establishing white supremacy on their plantations, those in the north were taking advantage of debts owed to them and the widespread desire to make it to Amerika. Through the use of indentured servants by the wealthy British colonizers in the Amerikas and West Indies, the labor of poor Irish people was exploited and used to accumulate wealth in much the same way as chattel slavery. However, contrary to the false rumors and irresponsible rhetoric you may have heard, Irish people were not then, nor were ever slaves.

The differences between chattel slavery and indentured servitude are vast enough to have significantly influenced the course of history. This influence had an impact that later helped to absorb Irish people into the white category of a society that was becoming increasingly racialized and white supremacist. While indentured servitude was indeed very brutal and torturous, it paled in comparison to that of chattel slavery. First of all, while indentured masters and slave masters both exploited the labor from those in their service, regularly inflicted physical and sexual violence, and mentally tortured those in their service to extract more labor and prevent uprisings, indentured servitude had a definite end. Indentured servants were only in bondage for a maximum of seven years. Enslaved peoples were born into and died while in chattel slavery. Second, once the contract for indentured servitude was fulfilled, either a debt was considered paid in full, or land and property were given to the former servant by the former master as compensation for their service. Enslaved peoples received *checks notes*... nothing. They got nothing. Even after slavery was deprivatized and reserved strictly for use by the state and federal government, those who were released from bondage received nothing for their labor or their family's labor or their ancestors labor before them. Some were even kidnapped and sold back into slavery by plantation owners who cared more about their profits than they did about the outcome of the Civil War or the laws that followed. Lastly, often times former indentured servants whose former masters decided not to fulfill their end of the indentured contract went down south to work on these plantations as overseers and slave catcher's. Although the plantation owners and their families were also abusive and degrading to the overseers, the Irish began to identify more with the masters than the slaves. Even though we had more in common with the slaves and had more to gain by allying ourselves with the enslaved people, our ancestors opted to go the self-serving route and instead aspired to achieve status and gratification by ingratiating ourselves into the good graces of the colonial aristocracy. Spoiler alert: the British colonists were just as disgusted by us as they were by Black people. They just saw the opportunity to use our sameness of skin color to get us to be the ones inflicting direct violence against enslaved Black people. But it would be centuries before they considered us white enough to be their equals. And they only did so as a way to further solidify their white supremacist society after slavery was deprivatized.

Irish people have indeed suffered at the hands of the British. Both in Amerika and in Ireland, British colonization took a very abusive toll on poor Irish people. But we have never been slaves. And our time spent under indentured servitude cannot be compared to the unconscionable and subhuman brutality inflicted upon Black people who were forced to endure the most egregious, despicable, abhorrent form of slavery the world has ever seen. To use Irish misfortune in order to erase the suffering of chattel slavery which left a long legacy of racism, marginalization, and more suffering is a disservice to the circumstances imposed upon both Irish and Black people as well as a blatantly ignorant attempt to hold on to your own racism.

Locs

Earlier, the book mentions dreadlocks as a form of cultural appropriation. Here, we will recap what we've learned as well as expand on statements that were made earlier. Let it be known, however, that whether we are referring to the origins of natural Black hair or we are discussing Black hairstyles in the modern context, white people who put dreadlocks in their hair are contributing to the erasure of Black culture which is a racist act. This is an inarguable fact.

If you know anything about history, then you know that the very first homo sapien appeared in Africa between 200,000 and 300,000 years ago. From her, humans evolved, as did societies. From primitive societies of humans came the first civilizations. The first civilizations to ever arise out of human existence were Egypt (then known as Kemet), Nubia (which began as a region of Kemet), and Sumeria. These civilizations were known as the Fertile Crescent. On a modern-day map, they stretched from what is now Iraq, Syria, and southwest down along the mouth of the Nile River through Egypt. While these regions may now be primarily Arab, they were originally Black civilizations and only became Arab through colonization which began nearly 5000 years after Egypt and Sumeria were first established. Arabization didn't begin until the 7th century B.C.E. and it took several more hundred years for the Arab language and identity to spread. From the earliest homo sapien to the start of Arabic colonization, all civilizations in and around Africa were Black. And it is from civilization that culture comes from. Stationary, non-nomadic societies of humans develop culture for communication, entertainment, expression, creation, and identity. The first known civilizations in human history were located in and along Africa. They were Black civilizations with Black culture.

The first known instances of locked hair date back to ancient Egypt. Depictions of people with locked hair appeared in art, hieroglyphics, and statues. Mummified Pharaohs were found buried with wigs that were locked. In ancient Mesopotamia, many of the Sumerians subscribed to the religion of Dagon. Dagon priests locked their hair as a show of commitment to the 77 commandments. Later, during British colonization of Africa in the 19th and 20th centuries, British soldiers were met by Kenyan warriors with locs in their hair. These locs evoked a deep sense of fear and dread in the British soldiers who then began to refer to the hairstyle as "dreadlocks". If culture is born out of civilizations and the first civilizations on earth were Black, then it stands to reason that the existence of locked hair in these civilizations is indeed Black culture.

Here, I'd like to point out that no, the Vikings did not have dreadlocks. The Vikings had braids and tangled hair. Because that's what happens to white hair when it goes unattended; it tangles. Black hair that's been left unattended locks. Naturally, on its own, if left alone, Black hair will lock up and grow into what we now call dreadlocks. This is known as "free forming". With free forming locs, Black hair will grow into differently sized locs and eventually turn into long plates of hair. White people's hair will tangle. And it will only tangle more the longer it's left on its own. This is why white people have to put so much work into getting our hair to clump up enough to form locs. We have to rat it, mat it, tease it, twist, and tie it. Some people even put chemicals like hairspray and gel in it. Others have gone as far as putting in foods like egg whites and ironing their hair just to get it to lock up. All Black people have to do is leave it alone.

For a more even style of locs, Black people can twist it between their fingers. This will keep their locks similar in size to each other. The care and maintenance of locs is a bit more work but, that's true for any hair style of any race. You know what happens when white people twist our hair between our fingers? Nothing. Nothing happens. Our hair doesn't lock up. Because it wasn't meant to. Don't believe me? Go ahead and try it. Twist your hair between your fingers for a while. See what happens.

However, for the sake of argument, let's say that locs don't originate from Black civilizations. Would they still be a Black hairstyle? Would white people still be appropriating culture if we put them in our hair? The answer to both of those questions is yes. Black people have consistently been ridiculed, degraded, and shamed by white society for what naturally grows out of their scalp. Particularly Black women have had to endure the subtle psychological terrorism that has been on repeat since at least the 1400's that white hair is the standard for beauty, hygiene, and acceptance. From the conk in the 40's and 50's to the hot comb and flat iron in the 80's and 90's, Black people have been made to feel like their natural hair is not straight enough, fine enough, clean enough, or light enough. However, as was so astutely pointed out earlier, Black hair naturally locks up. It is a naturally occurring hairstyle for Black people. Now that Black people are finally beginning to embrace their natural selves and reject what white society says is acceptable, white people want to take it for ourselves too.

Still, even if you do want to try dispute whether or not ancient white cultures wore locs or not one thing is for sure, it wasn't until the 1960's and 70's that white people even began wearing dreadlocks in the modern world. With the growing popularity of Bob Marley and the appeal that his radical approach to love had on white anti-Vietnam war activists, we decided that a great way to advertise our own political statement would be by appropriating that of the Rastafarian religion in which locs are a sacred symbol of the rejection of worldly materialism and a commitment to an all-natural lifestyle. What we do with them is use them as nothing more than props. To us, locs are simply a way for us to show our individuality. We use them to signify to society that we're edgy, rebellious, and non-conforming. And we're praised and respected by our peers for it.

However, even white people who try to claim their dreadlocks are symbolic of their conversion to the Rastafarian religion do so out of ignorance on the history of their own appropriated religion. Because Rastafarianism is, by definition, a religion founded on Black liberation through particular interpretations from the Bible. Therefore, there is no such thing as a white Rastafarian. There are only white perpetrators stealing aesthetics and using their affinity for reggae and Marijuana to try and legitimize their theft. You've turned the man who dared to love in the most radical way possible into nothing more than the poster boy for getting high and you've turned a sacred symbol into nothing more than a middle finger to your parents. You're a grown-up having an adult temper tantrum manifested as an identity crisis. Meanwhile, Black people are still stigmatized, criminalized, and alienated just for embracing a part of their actual identity. If you're white and you have dreadlocks, or cornrows, or any other Black hairstyle, then your entire identity is based on ignorance.

Critical Race Theory

Most people can't even tell you what critical theory is, let alone critical race theory. Simply put, critical theory is the philosophy that questioning everything, particularly our social institutions and how they've been established can lead to improving our society overall. All critical race theory does is adds race to that equation. Since the dawn of civilization, humanity's greatest minds have sought explanations and answers to life's most complex questions and enigmas. Questioning all the ways in which race has affected the establishment and development of our social institutions and functions is what critical race theory seeks to contribute in answering these questions. Offering explanations through a lens that, up until now, has been passed over and dismissed, despite being inarguably one of the largest contributing factors to the way our society has been constructed. And most of the people who are unable to explain what critical race theory is, or even critical theory, are opposed to implementing it into Amerika's education system.

What Isaac Newton publicized, and what the world's greatest thinkers knew long before he did, is that for every action, there is an equal and opposite reaction. This is an inescapable fact of life that explains many of life's once inexplicable phenomena. The psychological result to being abused is often to become abusive. A pendulum that is pulled will swing. A bell that is hit will ring. This is the natural order. Every action has a result. The condition of the U.S., the Black and Native communities in particular, is the results of chattel slavery, apartheid, and generational genocide. (Side note: I've specifically chosen not to use the word segregation because segregation implies equality and autonomy on both sides of which there was none for Black and Native people.) The rampant poverty, the economic disparities, the high rate of murder at the hands of police, the addiction epidemic, gang violence and street life, the decline of the nuclear family, the high rate of disease related to poor diet, and many other effects that plague the Black and Native communities at large are a social reaction. You don't get to have slavery for almost 300 years (600 if you count the first time Europeans established a slave trade in Africa. But I know most of the people reading this book don't think there is or don't care about a world outside of Amerika, so we'll just stick to what applies to the U.S.), apartheid for another at least 75, and genocide during the entire 500-year history of Europeans here, and then just "abolish", "integrate", and set aside some baron reservations and then think that everything is now okay. Centuries of chattel slavery and another nearly whole century of brutal apartheid along with the sustained genocidal practice against the Natives will necessarily and inevitably have repercussions that last, at the very least, as long as chattel slavery, Jim Crow, and the genocide did. Implementing critical race theory into the Amerikan education system offers a more thorough and objective explanation to the young minds of the future for how our society was started and why it is the way it is now.

Just to be clear, implementing critical race theory into the Amerikan school system would not be enough to make up for all the other ways that it upholds white supremacy. However, if critical race theory were to be applied, children would have a chance to learn a more complete history of the U.S. and not just the parts that shine a positive historical light on our presence as white people in a land that never belonged to us in the first place. Critical race theory would add slightly more balance to an education system that has been designed to uphold modern Amerikan society as the pinnacle of freedom and democracy by glorifying its origins. It would increase the possibility of kids drawing a conclusion about our current society that differs from what is meant for them to draw. And this is precisely why the white people who do understand critical race theory are so opposed to it.

What fails to be recognized by those who do not understand critical race theory is that the people who do understand it and oppose it, do so because they benefit from its absence in school. The inclusion of critical race theory in the education system is a direct threat to the power that politicians, lobbyists, CEO's, Wall Street bankers, trust fund billionaires, and all those who make the decisions for society are able to keep through your patriotism and commitment to traditional Amerikan ideals and institutions. However, more often than not, this benefit does not also extend to those who do not understand critical race theory. When the leaders and politicians that you support and identify with are opposed to something, it is not a cue for you to automatically adopt that same opinion. Having politicians, pundits, and social leaders who influence and make our decisions for us does not absolve us of the responsibility to think for ourselves. Opposing things that we ourselves do not understand just because other people we politically agree with do, is ignorant; and lazy. I'm hoping that by the time you read this book, this section at least, if not the entire book, will no longer be relevant to society. But I genuinely believe that the only way critical race theory would ever get taught in school is if every other main point discussed in this book is also became no longer relevant to society.

Black-on-Black Crime

It is the coinciding reality of street culture intersecting with Black culture that racists use to justify certain racist ideas they have. When a racist equates Black behavior with a ghetto mentality it is because Black culture and street culture intersect. It is racism that makes these two cultures intersect. Therefore, it is racism that equates one to the other. Black culture is conflated with street culture because street life was created for the survival of poverty. Street culture grew out of the crimes that were committed to survive being poor. However, these crimes eventually became common place due to the persistence of poverty. As these crimes grew in popularity due to their ability to offer instant survival against the sure death of poverty, they eventually began to develop a culture of their own. This culture influenced the thought process and mind set of those who had the most exposure to them and the inevitable attraction to the street life was born. The greater the poverty, the stronger the attraction. And it is Black people who have been systematically kept impoverished.

Conversely, most of the so-called "ghetto" culture is just Black culture that white people have demonized. It's a culture that they have built up from nothing in order to survive poverty by keeping in touch with themselves. Because so called ghetto culture and street culture are both derived from being kept in a perpetual state of poverty, racists use that as an opportunity to equate the two, assert their racism, and then try to justify it without feeling like a racist.

This racist mentality is then taken a step further when racists use the term "Black-on-Black crime" to rationalize the police murder of Black people. When the Black community comes together to protest the obvious murder of one of their own at the hands of police, those of us who defy the protests will often use the "Black-on-Black crime" narrative to try and excuse what is an obvious lynching. Yet, there are two glaring contradictions with using the "Black-on-Black crime" justification for murder.
First, there is no such thing as "Black-on-Black crime". It's just crime. The same way there's no such thing as white-on-white crime, asian-on-asian crime, or any other exclusively ethnic crime statistic. You never hear about any other racially exclusive crime phenomena to justify those killings, or in any context for that matter. The only time that phrase is even ever used is in reference to the Black community. Furthermore, crime occurs in a matter of proximity. This is a proven fact. Which is precisely why white people who commit crimes do so against other white people at a very similar rate as Black people of between 80 and 90%. To suggest that Black-on-Black crime is an objective phenomenon is to imply that Black people are inherently more violent and criminal than any other race. Try saying that without sounding racist.

Second, even if there were such thing as Black-on-Black crime, that still does not justify the police murder of Black people. Suggesting that it is okay for police to kill Black people because they kill each other is using the same logic as saying that it is okay for terrorists to kill Amerikans because Amerikans kill each other. If you still think "Black-on-Black crime" is a valid argument for supporting the flagrant murder of Black people at the hands of police, then your ignorance is not only racist, but also a conscious decision you've made to remain so.

The Black Experience

Also, earlier in the book, we discussed white arrogance. The mentality that some of us have which makes us think we automatically know better than Black and brown people and are the de facto authority on all

matters. This mindset and the assertion of it shine through in the prevalence of our propensity to tell Black people about their own experiences in Amerika. We then take our arrogance to the next level by telling Black people how they should deal with their own experiences in Amerika.
Not everyone in Amerika has the same experience. Neither does everyone in Amerika experience it the same. It's extremely naive and narrow minded to think that everyone has the same relationship world as we do. So too is it narrow-minded to think that everyone has the same circumstances and opportunities as we do. This mentality required the assumption that the world sees and treats us all equally. It also has the very naive implication that we all have an equal amount of power over our own lives. Both of which are grossly untrue.

There's not a whole lot that I can say to the Black experience in Amerika because I'm not Black. I can, however, tell you that, because I'm not Black, I have no right to tell Black people about their own experiences. Nor do I have the right to tell them how to deal with those experiences. We're not Black. We'll never be Black. Our ancestors were never enslaved in this country. Nor were they paid for their labor after they were let go. Our ancestors' families weren't purposely torn apart, children taken from their mothers and sold off to a plantation hundreds of miles away, some even used for alligator bait which obviously would have resounding effects on the mental stability of any mother. The men and women raped and tortured which they eventually ended up bringing into their homes and passed down from generation to generation and then blamed for the dissolution of the family. Our grandparents never had to endure life with the constant fear of lynch mobs, the humiliation of constant submission to any white person under threat of the law, or the incessant psychological degradation of their appearances the effects of which would also be handed down from generation to generation. Our parents weren't the intentional target of a direct attack on our people by the government to flood our neighborhoods with crack cocaine wreaking havoc on our community, turning brothers and sisters into drug addicts, fathers into dealers and mothers into prostitutes. Then locked away for it. Doing time in prison for sentences 100 times longer than white people for cocaine, which is literally the same drug as crack. Crack is made from cocaine. Yet the sentence for getting busted with crack is 100 to 1. For every 1 day that a person who gets busted with cocaine spends in prison, a person who gets busted with crack spends 100. Our leaders have never been gunned down in public, subjected to government surveillance programs, targeted by FBI operations, and made a spectacle of. They've never systematically eliminated every servant of our people who tried to improve our conditions. We've never had to live in constant fear of police, been unfairly accused of wrongdoing, been seen through the eyes of the law as adults when we're just kids, and never even allowed to explore our limits and just have the same fun as other kids without being vilified and criminalized for it. We've never had to face the prospect of a 75% chance that we'll end up in prison despite being only 13% of the population. And never, ever, ever have we had to endure the social and psychological effects of any of that while still being expected to maintain a fully functional adult life under white supremacist capitalism.

So, it's important for us to gain some humility, shut up, and listen if and when Black people are gracious enough to share their experiences with us. Because if they do, they're actually teaching us a lot about the world. They're offering us new perspectives to life that can help us gain a much more comprehensive understanding of it. Because the arrogance that it takes to tell someone else they're wrong about their own relationship with the world is nauseatingly ignorant.

Victim Blaming

For some of us, it's easier to blame the dead person for being dead than it is to admit what killed them. Because for some of us, admitting what killed them would either be a direct threat to how we believe the world works or it would be equal to an outright admission of our racism. However, the latter, of course, would require the realization that we are, in fact, racist.

Some white people refuse to realize that our society is not a uniform place; that not every outcome is guaranteed for everyone by the making the same decision. In fact, some of us even have the audacity to foretell outcomes that never happened, and likely would not have given the other circumstances involved. We actually believe that we know better how to deal with certain situations than the people who were in them. We question why this person didn't do what we believe they should have done. Then, worst of all, we follow it up with the explanation that if they had, their outcome would have been more favorable for them.

There are also some of us who believe that the accusation of a crime - any crime - is enough to warrant an instant death sentence. The idea that the slightest infraction of a rule justifies the wonton death of Black people is precisely fascist. Suggesting that a person refrain from breaking the law to avoid death is Nazism; the highest level of fascism.

If we don't wish to subscribe to the fascist ideology, then we need to understand a few things about how a democratic society is supposed to work, even if it is a sham of a democracy. We need to understand that the penalty for failing to comply with an officer's orders is not a firing squad. We must understand that the penalty for resisting arrest is not the electric chair. We have to understand that the penalty for stealing a candy bar or using counterfeit money is not lethal injection. We must come to terms with the fact that police are not supposed to make the decision of who is guilty and who is not. Furthermore, we have got to understand that, even if they are caught in the middle of committing a crime, that police are still not justified in killing them. Understand that Black people have just as much right to bear arms as white people. Understand that a Black person with a gun is no more dangerous than a white person with a gun. Understand that if a Black person were actually reaching for a cop's gun, it is most likely an impulsive attempt to prevent the cop from using it. Because cops are much more notorious for killing Black people than Black people are of taking a cop's gun to use it. But also understand that it is highly unlikely that anyone would be able to remove a cop's gun from its holster given the safety mechanisms in place specifically for such an event. Understand that it is even less likely that the Black person was actually reaching for the cop's gun.

Attempting to use any one or more of these excuses is an implicit adherence to the idea that unquestioning submission to authority constitutes two things. First, that unquestioning obedience can coexist with democracy. Second, the unquestioning submission to authority will guarantee the safety of Black people. Both are categorically false. Unquestioning submission to authority is fascist. And just like it didn't in Nazi Germany for Jewish people, submission does not guarantee safety for Black people. To assert any one of these excuses in the event of a Black person's murder at the hands of police, is automatically a subscription to Nazism. Because that was the difference between fascism and Nazism. Fascism is the supreme authority of one ruling political party. Nazism was the supreme authority of one ruling political party with an emphasis on the subjugation and extermination of people which the aforementioned political party deemed "undesirable". In other words, blatant, outright fascist. Unfortunately, due to the widespread misinformation and authoritative conditioning that our population has received, many white people are completely bereft of the realization that victim blaming is fascist. And doing so in the context of a Black person being murdered by a white person or an agent of the white power structure, is neo-Nazism. The failure to realize that excusing murder through fascist rationale in a so-called de-mocracy necessarily constitutes racism, is ignorant. The failure to admit and own up to it is willful ignorance.

The Real Difference

Honestly, I absolutely hate that I have to write this section. It infuri-ates me that the ignorance of my people requires me to even think about this word, let alone imply it. It enrages me even more that the ignorance of my people has placed me in the position of having to think about and analyze such a lazy, repugnant mindset. Nevertheless, being that some of us still have such narrow minded and ignorant views, the need for this section is greater than my disdain for it.

Unfortunately, coming from a racist family, I've heard a lot of igno-rant things said about Black, Brown, Native and Asian people. However, one of, if not the, most ignorant thing I've ever heard was that there was a difference between a Black person and a - - - - er. This statement is often used by white people regarding Black people who display any behavior we disapprove of. When a Black person does something to upset or of-fend a white person, this statement is often a go-to statement as a way of verbalizing our racism which tends to be accentuated by anger, with-out feeling like a racist. We think that if we can differentiate between the Black people we approve of and the ones that we don't, then our failure to classify all Black people as a - - - - er exempts us of being racist. How-ever, the fact that we think we have the right to control or validate Black people's behavior in the first place is already racist.

The idea that there is a difference between a Black person and a - - - - er means that our idea of an acceptable Black person is one who be-haves only in ways that suit us. This mentality is usually directed towards Black people who refuse to take a submissive attitude towards us. This implies that we believe Black people are required to model themselves after what white people have deemed appropriate. That is the epitome of white supremacist. Black people are not required to make us feel com-fortable in order to be valid human beings. Telling a Black person that they're "one of the good ones" is not a compliment. It means that we see Black people as inferior to us. We see the ones who make us uncomfort-able as inferior specifically because they assert their humanity by choos-ing to act however they want. This upsets us because we believe our ex-pectations to take precedence over their autonomy. We see the ones who do not make us uncomfortable as inferior because we believe that being passive and docile is an attempt to gain our approval acceptance.

We assume that they are placing our expectations and feelings above their autonomy because they see us as important and superior as we see ourselves.

Thinking that Black people should behave in a way that makes you comfortable is not just ignorant, it's also arrogant. Being arrogant in your ignorance is not just racist, it's also pathetic. The real difference is that you think you've found a loophole to avoid being racist, but you've only actually managed to find another way to be racist.

If You Don't Like It, Why Don't You Just Leave

One of the most ignorant, and quite frankly, downright stupidest arguments that racists use when the white supremacist nature of Amerika is pointed out, is that if you don't like it here, you can leave. This argument is so bereft of logic and intelligent thought that it could only come from someone who is not accustomed to using their brain. There are three main reasons why this logic is an absolute failure.

First of all, there's always room for improvement. The take-it-or-leave-it argument places the condition of the U.S. in an unsuitable context that implies the need for people to settle for their current reality. Telling people to settle for their current state of affairs in life technically goes against everything that Amerika claims to stand for. Even if Amerika was the greatest country in the world, it still would not absolve us of the responsibility to make it better.

Second of all, this is precisely the type of mentality that capitalism breeds. The self-centered, dog-eat-dog, overly competitive, one against all, win at all costs approach to life prevents those who believe in it from understanding why anyone would want to stay somewhere they're unhappy with because they're unable to think past their own self interests. However, contrary to the entire premise of Amerikanization, doing so wouldn't do anything to help remedy anyone else's situation except your own. Leaving the place you've lived your entire life because it's violent and oppressive toward you and your people may help you, but it still leaves everyone else you love there to suffer. When you inherit a house from your parents and the plumbing is going bad, you don't abandon the house. You fix the plumbing.

Lastly, where are they going to go? Where would someone who hypothetically wanted to leave Amerika go? There's nowhere in the world that hasn't been affected in one way or another by western ideology, Amerikan imperialism and anti-Black racism. If not through overthrown democratically elected governments and Amerikan interested puppet regimes, then by predatory natural resource companies and the daily bombing of innocent citizens. If not through the culture of assimilation and gluttonous consumerism then through the extortion of the International Monetary Fund and overly cautious, authoritative governments trying to maintain their national sovereignty by preventing all of the above. Not to mention supporting outright fascist regimes including Afghanistan in the 80's, Brazil, the Pinochet dictatorship in Chile, Albania, the Batista dictatorship in Cuba, ousting Nkrumah in Ghana, Indonesia, Anastasia Somosa of Nicaragua, and many more. In fact, the former U.S.S.R., Cuba, Iran, and North Korea are the way they are because Amerika can't keep its own greed contained within its own borders. The U.S. has successfully overthrown governments in 37 countries just since the end of WWII. And has attempted at least double that. In Latin America alone the U.S. has performed 56 official "interventions" and backed 16 right-wing military coups. That's not including any of the ones in the middle east like Iran or in Asia like South Korea. The U.S. has been either directly or indirectly involved in countless successful assassinations including Patrice Lumumba of the Congo, Salvador Allende and General Renee Schneider of Chile, Muammar Gaddafi of Libya, and Ngo Dinh Diem of South Vietnam with many more attempted all throughout Africa, Asia, the Middle East, and Latin America including a total of 638 attempts just on Fidel Castro alone. There's nowhere to go that hasn't been negatively impacted by the Amerikan Imperial Empire.

If anyone who uses that argument in response to the assertion of Amerika's racism knew anything about history or anything besides what they're told to think, they would understand how feeble and moronic that argument really is. However, that's what happens when your Amerikan exceptionalism clouds your ability to think. You end up living in your own bubble with the impression that nothing exists outside of it. When nothing outside your own personal bubble is relevant to you, you start to make claims and judgements that are completely illogical and devoid of any context that you personally are unable to relate to.

Black People Are Not a Monolith

Finding a Black person that shares your views doesn't make you any less racist. Using Candace Owens or Ben Carson as a token to validate your racism only serves to further expose it by highlighting the fact that you think one Black person's views are representative of the entire community. Believe it or not, Black people are just as dynamic and diverse as every other human community. With different beliefs, opinions, and out-looks on life, Black people are not required to fit their humanity into a box just so you can understand them. However, when the majority of that community is saying something that contradicts what you believe, finding someone from that community to validate your belief is heading in the wrong direction. Doing research to support your opinions is backwards, illogical, and a disservice to those who you claim you're not racist against. The idea is to form your opinion based on your research. When white people seek out Black voices that we agree with, it's precisely so that we can justify our racist views as not racist. But remember, our ancestors tried to convince Black people that slavery was good for them. And there were some who believed it. But that didn't make it true. Just because Black people cannot be racist doesn't mean they cannot uphold racism. White supremacy does not require someone to be white in order to support it.

When we support our racist attitudes with that of Black people who agree with us, we are intentionally seeking out tokens to validate our racism which itself makes us racist. This ignorance comes from the fear of admitting that we have racist ideas. Instead of doing better and educating ourselves out of racism, we hold on to our ignorance by finding a Black spokesperson to validate us and position them as an authority on all things Black. Both of which are ignorant attempts to rationalize our racism

The Default Race

Some of us have such a paralyzing fear of being seen as racist that in order to present the image that we are non-racist to the world, we do things that more accurately reflect our misunderstanding of racism than disprove it. By illuminating our misunderstanding of racism, how it works, and how its applied, we end up showing the entire world that our misunderstanding of racism is, in fact, what makes us racist. By doing things like whispering the words "Black", "African", "African-American", "Colored" or any other obvious descriptive word, or even avoiding using them alto-gether, we demonstrate an idea that racism will only occur if we offend a Black person. This presents two separate, but intersecting misconceptions and instances of racism.

First, by going to such ridiculous lengths to avoid offending Black peo-ple, we're essentially implying the belief that there is something wrong with being Black. In the year 2021, I've literally had someone who was telling me a story about something that happened to them say, "I'm not trying to be mean but, he was Black...". The fact that the man in the anecdote was Black was indeed relevant to the story however, just mentioning that he was Black is not what made the story or the storyteller racist. It's when the storyteller prefaced it with an unnecessary disclaimer about their intention for describing him as Black that it became racist. Such a disclaimer is born out of a fear of offending Black people and that this supposed offense will then leave us in place to be judged as racist. The fear itself is rooted in the idea that Black people need white sympathy.

What white people need to understand is that being Black is not an affliction, disease, pathology, deviation, or something to be ashamed of. Showing sympathy for Black people on the basis that they're Black is racist. There is more shame in feeling sorry for someone that they're Black than there is in being Black. The Black struggle is not Black people's fault. It's not that Black people need to be born white in order to ease the struggle of racism. It's that white people need to stop being racist.

The second misconception that whispering physical descriptions or intentionally omitting them altogether presents is the equation of these descriptions with the "N" word. When we see Black people getting upset and checking white people for using the "N" word, it's because of the history that word contains. White people used that word for centuries as a way to dehumanize, subjugate, and psychologically terrorize Black people in order to further enforce our oppressive relationship with them. As a means to fight back and dilute the power of that word, Black people adopted it and began to use it amongst each other. Whether it worked or not is not for white people to decide. In any case, the "N" word does not have the same meaning when used in and between the Black community. However, what we need to understand is that the "N" word now belongs to Black people. They paid for it, it's theirs. Any time a white person uses that word it reverts right back to its original intent. Therein lies the reason for Black people's offense and anger at white people using the "N" word. When white people whisper the words "Black", "African-American", etc. under our breath, or avoid using them at all, the misconception that it will offend Black people implies that we still equate them with the "N" word. The idea that Black people will be offended by referring to them as Black or African American indicates our own belief that being Black is equal to being the "N" word. All of which insinuates that we still consider them inferior to us. We still equate them to the "N" word, but we don't hate them for that, we feel sorry for them that they were born that way.

White people need to understand that white is not the default race. Being Black is not an affliction or a reason to assert our sympathy. Using skin pigment to describe a Black person is not racist. Feeling sorry for Black people for being Black and equating them with the inferior nature that birthed the "N" word, whether its malicious or sympathetic, exemplifies the type of ignorance that allows racism to persist without our awareness.

Black Power

Black power is a response to white power. It cannot possibly be equal to white power if it is the existence and imposition of white power that necessitates it. If it weren't for blatant white supremacists calling for white power and asserting their genocidal ideology, there would have been no need or desire for Black power. Trying to equate Black power with white power is a massive failure in understanding the state of Amerika. The demand for white power is necessarily a threat of violence. White power inherently implies the belief and desire to see anyone who is not white in a position of subjugation to, or extermination by, those who are. As such, the call for Black power is a survival response from this imminent threat. Black power is not anti-white. You just think it is because white power is anti-Black.

White Washing

Effectively, our whole society has been created by Black people. Not just the wealth and the infrastructure but, the culture as well. From cartoons to music to cultural icons. PBS has since confirmed that Betty Boop was actually inspired by a Black woman. In 1930, cartoonist Max Fleischer modeled Betty Boop after Harlem Jazz singer Esther Jones whose stage name was "Baby Esther". When the character was introduced, no one had any idea that the first animated sex symbol originated from Black people.

One of Amerika's most influential and iconic real life sex symbols was Marilyn Monroe. With her curvacious body, her soft bedroom eyes and sultry voice, she drove Amerika wild. Every man wanted her, and every woman wanted to be her, or so we've been told. What we aren't told is that her entire existence of fame rested on the shoulders of a Black woman. Marylin Monroe respected and idolized Dorothy Dandridge. Her whole style, appearance and sex appeal was directly influenced and modeled after Dorothy Dandridge, a Black woman.

He's known as the "King of Rock-N-Roll". His southern drawl, his sneered lip, and his unmistakable leg shake launched him into infamy as well as the Rock-N-Roll Hall of Fame. However, if it weren't Black people like Chuck Berry, Bo Diddley, and Rosetta Tharp, Elvis Presley would have been just another racist redneck.

From the ancient genius of African civilizations like Egypt to the sacred image of a man whose supposed divinity created the largest religion in the world and lived in Asia minor, white Amerika has been kept ignorant of white washing in order to maintain it. When we indulge in these past times or revere these symbols that have been whitewashed, we allow our ignorance to complete the white washing. By completing the white washing, we engage in the erasure of a culture that does not belong to us and further suppress the people that culture does belong to.

Blacks Sold Blacks Into Slavery

Let's just be real here, the only reason anyone would bring that up is to try and justify slavery. First of all, the practice of slavery in Africa was much different. Slaves in Africa were prisoners of war. They weren't unexpectedly kidnapped from the shores of their homeland and robbed of their entire identity. They may have been slaves, but they were still allowed to keep their names, their language, their music, their religion, and the rest of their culture. Second of all, when the Europeans showed up to start kidnapping and enslaving Black people, European colonization and imperialism had already begun to ravage the continent. European capitalism had already spread throughout Africa placing African slave traders in the very precarious position of having to survive an economic system that was being built to oppress them. I'm not even going to go into more detail because the level of ignorance in that argument is enough to induce severe migraines.

Ignorance is bliss. Ignorance is comfortable. Ignorance is also inexcusable. We live in the age of information. If there's something you want to know, there's no excuse for not knowing it. When it comes to racism in the 21st century, the amount of discourse and conflict about racism that has been thrust into the public eye is undeniable. If the BLM movement has done nothing else, it has certainly brought race into the forefront of many conversations that it previously would have been left out of. The global public, and the Amerikan public in particular, have been inundated with real life events, parallel story lines, controversies, characters, uncovered scandals, and shameful viral videos on social media enough to realize the relevance and urgency of this topic. There is virtually no way anyone can deny at least a cursory awareness of how prevalent the topic of racism is. Choosing to believe previously held ideas that are being debunked and disproven is nothing more than a commitment to misunderstanding. This commitment is brought on by incentivized opposition. Opposing a point of view or holding onto old, outdated ones in order to maintain a level of comfort to which we've become accustomed offers us enough reason to stay in the dark. In the book The Republic by Plato, he offers an allegory known as "The Cave". The allegory states that there exist prisoners chained together in a cave. Behind the prisoners is a fire, and between the fire and the prisoners are people carrying puppets or other objects. This casts a shadow on the other side of the wall which the prisoners watch and believe them to be real. Plato suggests that one prisoner could get free, see the fire, and realize the shadows are fake. This prisoner could then escape from the cave and discover there is a whole new world outside that they were previously unaware of. This prisoner would believe the outside world is so much more real than that in the cave. He would try to return to free the other prisoners however, upon his return, he is blinded because his eyes are not accustomed to actual sunlight. The chained prisoners would then see this blindness and believe they will be harmed if they try to leave the cave. Ignorance is a commitment to denying the uncomfortable reality in favor of a comfortable lie.

Chapter 17
Welfare

We just love to judge them, don't we? It makes us feel superior and righteous. Even if it's just in our minds, judging people who are on welfare is an instant boost to our own self esteem. It doesn't even matter if we don't know for sure whether or not they're on it, we have our preconceived notions of what someone on welfare looks like. Then when we see someone who fits our preconceived profile, our judgements towards them become automatic. When we're alone in our homes or with our close circle of associates, and the topic arises, we apply these judgements to a hypothetical version of what we think someone on welfare looks like. Some of us don't even make an effort to hide it. We'll flat out admit that we think Black women with more than one kid or who is separated from the child's father must be on welfare.

I think that what we need to do first is figure out why so many of us have such a problem with people on welfare in the first place. And honestly, the answer to that is really a very simple one. We've spent nearly 300 years listening to politicians talk in and out of their mouths about taxes. There most likely isn't a single working or middle class person alive that hasn't gotten upset about how much money the government takes from them at one point or another. Most, if not at all of us felt the shock of that injustice the most when we got our very first paycheck from our very first job. That feeling was so intense that, whether or not we're prepared to admit it, it stuck with us subconsciously for the rest of our lives. So now, if there is one political issue that we all care about, it's how much money is going to be coming out of paychecks.

Then we found out that welfare and food stamps are funded by the taxes that come out of our checks. Naturally this upset us. It seemed to us that if they didn't have to fund food stamps and welfare with our taxes then that would mean they would take less money out of our paychecks for taxes. But the only way that was going to happen is if the people who were using food stamps and welfare stopped doing so. So, we took a look to see who exactly all our tax money was going to. The answer to that was pretty obvious too. Clearly it was going to poor people. Or at least that's what we've been led to believe. And, since we'd also been conditioned to believe that poverty is a personal failure rather than an integral part of our economy, we began to blame the poorer people in our society. It seemed to us that if they would just get a job and stop sitting around on their lazy butts or having so many kids that the system is required to help them, then we could get more of the money that we work so hard for.

Well, since, as previously mentioned, Black people have been systematically kept in a state of poverty ever since they were first kidnapped from the shores of Africa, our disdain inevitably turned to them. We slandered them for being lazy, we labeled them deadbeats, we accused them of abusing the system and, ultimately, we blamed them for the amount of money that was being taken out of our paychecks. We concocted all kinds of assumptions that were overtly classist but with not-so-subtle racist undertones in order to satisfy our feelings of virtuous superiority and justify our arrogance. We felt like they were profiting off of all our hard work. How ironic that we still glorify rich people.

However, this self-righteous crusade against poor Black people was misguided from the very beginning. The logic that guided the decision to aim our anger at poor Black people was inconsistent, full of holes, and unduly influenced. When we heard politicians argue about where our tax dollars should be going, the subject of the argument invariably included just how much should be going to poor people. News stories were always reporting on these social security programs. Even presidents would get on television to paint the image of a quintessential welfare queen in our heads. But we never heard politicians argue about how much of our tax money should be going to corporate subsidies. News pundits never discussed how much Politicians should be paying themselves. Presidents never got on TV to discuss how much should be going to the defense budget or to major oil companies. Unless you regularly tune in to CSPAN, the only stories the average person hears about are whether or not our taxes should help poor people. The circumstances this seemingly intentional omission created has obscured and distorted a few key facts that, if left plain and clear, would drastically shift our perception of tax money allocation.

Fact 1. Virtually every time these other issues are raised in congress, it's pretty much unanimous. On both sides of the aisle, the vote to pad the "defense" budget to $778 billion dollars for the year 2020 was an emphatic "yes". The U.S. spends more on "defense" than the next top 11 countries combined. The country with the second highest defense budget is China at $252 billion. That's about 1/3 of what the U.S. spends. The instruments of death and destruction have reached costs that far exceed anything even remotely resembling defense. The no-bid contracts that the government offers to weapons manufacturers are essentially a blank check for these warlords to create the most advanced killing machines imaginable. And with a no-bid contact, their only competition is themselves. They have only to create deadlier, more efficient, more impersonal, more blood thirsty, more destructive, more sadistic, and more expensive weapons than the one they did before. The Trident II missile is a ballistics missile that is fired from a submarine and armed with nuclear warheads. This missile system is employed by both the U.S. and the British navy. However, we are the only 2 nations in the world with them. Each missile system costs around $26.6 billion each. How is forcing every single nation in the world to live under the constant threat of certain annihilation at the whim of the U.S. considered defense and not bullying? The F-35 fighter jet is the most expensive weapon in the world. Initially, when it first came off the production line in 2007, it cost $220 million. Due to a multitude of problems with its programing, that number dropped to around $77.9 million. Today, upfront costs are between $100 and $110 million. However, over the course of its lifetime, operation and maintenance costs will skyrocket to a staggering $1.7 trillion. All of which will be coming from taxpayers. For the record, if we were to buy every single homeless person in the U.S. a $600,000 house, it would cost around $331.6 billion. That's only about 1/5 the cost of just one F-35 fighter jet. And that's money being spent on helping people to live rather than an overpriced weapon to kill them.

Fact 2. SNAP or the Supplement Nutrition Assistance Program, which is the modern equivalent of food stamps, cost the average Amerikan taxpayer between $200 and $300 a month. Corporate subsidies cost the average taxpayer between $500 and $650 a month. These subsidies are in addition to any and all profits that they make. Between 1978 and 2020, CEO salaries have increased by over 900%. And that's just their salaries. That doesn't even include the bonuses they give themselves. You don't think your tax dollars have helped to fund the obscene increase in CEO bank accounts with the subsidies they get from the federal government? Have you ever heard of a CEO that regularly takes their suit coat off, unbuttons their cuff links, rolls their sleeves up and works shoulder-to-shoulder with any of their employees? No. Of course not. Not on any kind of regular basis anyway. Not unless cameras are around to capture it as a public relations stunt or inspiration porn.

Fact 3. Similarly, all members of congress in both the house and the senate make $175,000 a year. That alone would be $93.6 million however, that doesn't include the speaker's salary which is over $220,000 a year or the majority and minority leaders which are over $190,000 a year. Between 2007 and 2021, congress met for an average of 158 days per year. Keep in mind that this annual congressional workday count does not include any of the times that senators and congress people have been photographed literally sleeping on the job. In contrast, the average working-class person works around 260 days a year.

Fact 4. It's no secret that, as previously stated multiple times, Black people have been systematically kept in a state of poverty. However, what's not quite as well known is that there are more white people on welfare than Black people. Nearly 40% of SNAP recipients are white while just over 25% are Black. However, contrary to racist and classist beliefs, about 70% of the people who are on SNAP and Medicaid work full time jobs. Now before you go blaming these people for abusing and taking advantage of the system, it should be noted that quite the opposite is true. It's their employers who are abusing and taking advantage of the system. The national average wage that Walmart pays their employees is $16.40 an hour. However, their minimum wage, which was just increased by a dollar earlier in 2021, is $12 an hour. Which means people start out at $12 an hour and work their way up to $16. Furthermore, $16.40 an hour is just over $34,000 a year. In the U.S., the average monthly rent for a 1-bedroom apartment is $1,100. At $16.40 an hour for 40 hours a week, gross monthly pay is $2,624. The recommended formula, and in most cases, the rental company's minimum requirements for renting an apartment is to make at least 3 times what your monthly rent is. At $16.40 an hour for full time, rent would have to be around $875 a month.

Fact 5. Walmart happens to be the largest employer in the U.S. with over 2.2 million workers. Walmart also receives a yearly subsidy from the federal government of $6.2 billion. Even if they paid every single one of their 2.2 million employees a reasonable, livable $30 an hour wage, that's still only $66 million. In order for employee wages to take up the entire $6.2 billion that they receive from the federal government, Walmart would have to pay every single employee almost $94 an hour. And this doesn't even count any of the $559 billion in 2021 profits that Walmart made as the largest retailer in the U.S.

Oh, you thought this might be anomalous!? Like this is just exclusive to Walmart? Oh no. In fact, McDonald's and Target, who are both also 2 of the largest employers in the U.S., follow the same trend. Their subsidies come from state taxes rather than federal, and vary slightly from state to state however, since 2003, McDonald's has accumulated over $7.3 billion and Target $177 million since 2001. The national average wage for McDonald's employees is $10.68 an hour and for Target is $14 an hour. For Amazon, their subsidies have grown to $3.7 billion since 2016. And that's just the ones that are traceable. In 2020, the median wage for an Amazon employee wasn't even $30,000 a year. The oil industry receives $20.5 billion a year in subsidies from both state and federal governments.

Comparatively, is estimated that SNAP and Medicaid cost $153 billion just between Walmart and McDonald's employees. This pattern of greed and abuse is also found at Burger King, Wendy's, Taco Bell, Home Depot, Lowe's, Walgreens and CVS. Now before you go regurgitating the absurdly ridiculous idea that these people should have gone to college to get a higher paying job, there's a few things you may want to consider. Fact 6. Since the year 2000, the in-state cost of tuition at a 4-year university has increased by 80%. Since 1990, it has increased 130% when adjusted for inflation. In the same time frame, the real cost of wages has increased by only 3%. People with "some college experience" in 2019 are just now starting to exceed the "some college experience" wages of 2007.

Fact 7. If these people did all get better paying jobs, there would be no one to ring up your groceries, no one for you to curse out when they won't take your expired coupon, no one to stock the shelves with merchandise for you to gorge your gluttonous indulgences with, no one to look down on for making a mistake while filling your orders, and no one to make your cheeseburgers when you're too lazy to cook. There would be no one left for you hurl your entitlements and aim your adult temper tantrums at. Because if these jobs really were just for high school age kids, you would throw a fit when you couldn't get your daily latte during school hours. Everyone deserves a wage they can live on. Even the people you degrade take yourself feel superior. Because otherwise, what's the point of having a job? But until everyone is given a fair wage for their hard labor, they still need to eat, and they still need health care.

So, what have we learned from these facts? Well, for starters, If you're worried about people who don't work getting your tax money to fund their extravagant lifestyles, then either you're mad at the wrong people for the wrong reasons or you're using the necessity for social safety nets as a cover to assert your racism so that you can be racist without being called racist. Secondly, there are more white people on welfare than there are Black people. So, now you no longer have a cover nor euphemism for your racism. Third, the defense budget has reached proportions so large that it can no longer be accurately referred to as a "defense budget". It would be more appropriate to describe it as a world conquest budget. And it's funded by all of your hard work. Fourth, corporate subsidies cost taxpayers much more than welfare does. However, the corporations, obviously, need it much less than the welfare recipients do. Fifth, the need for any welfare at all is, in large part, due to the unfettered greed and systemic abuse from corporate interests. These corporations take money from both your right and left pocket. They drastically enlarge the need for social welfare by their workers due to paying them so little on the one hand. And on the other hand, they rake in their subsidies that the state and federal governments use your taxes for and add it to their already overstuffed pockets. You're worried about poor people abusing and taking advantage of the same system that rich people do. Yet, you only get upset when poor people do it because you think it's stealing but, when rich people do it, it's considered good business.

If you haven't figured it out by now, it doesn't matter what social welfare programs are in place, they're never going to take less money out of your check. They will always find a place for your money to go that doesn't benefit you or your community. It's ironic how not once did we think to direct our anger toward those who were actually taking the money out of our paycheck but, instead to those who we thought that money was going to. But, at least with social welfare, I know that it's going to people who actually need it rather than some rapacious captain of industry or grimy oil tycoon that already has more money than he knows what to do with and made it all by paying his employees starvation wages. I would rather $100 of my dollars go to people who are "too lazy" to work than $1 of my dollars not go to someone with 2 jobs and 3 hungry kids. But if you can't say the same, then congratulations! You've managed to successfully merge your racism with your classism.

Chapter 18
(Un)Acceptable Forms of Protest

Imagine there's a problem in Amerika. It's a problem that has been pervasive and destructive for centuries. It affects everyone of a particular community on a daily basis. The immediate threat that this problem poses is both sudden and ever present at the same time. The contradiction of this problem's existence is enough to keep anyone on perpetual edge. Not everyone in Amerika acknowledges the problem but, the vast majority of the community that is affected understands and is acutely aware of it. The repetitive pleas, the incessant requests, and the persistent demands to fix and end this problem have all largely fallen on deaf ears. The cries for help from those that live under its constant threat have gone unheard or denied altogether. By and large, the lawmakers and policy writers refuse to acknowledge the problem. Those who do acknowledge it swear their hands are tied. There always seems to be something that bars them from taking action. It's always someone else's responsibility. Its always excuse after excuse, restraint after restraint. In fact, the so-called justice system actually works in the problem's favor to ensure the maintenance of the problem's severity.

Or, maybe there's a policy being proposed that could impact the lives of every single person in the country. The proposal of this policy has essentially placed everyone on one side or the other. Some people agree with the policy. They believe it is in the best interest of the country. They feel it would benefit everyone. These people feel that this policy is the answer to a deadly problem that puts every person in the world at risk. And if this policy were to be put in place, it could help everyone in the country, and even the world, get back to a sense of normalcy. Or at least mitigate the looming threat of contracting a disease that has proven to be fatal.

Others believe that this policy is an imposition on their personal freedom. They feel that a policy mandating everyone to have something done to their body whether or not they agree with it is not only a personal violation but, also a dangerous precedent to set. These people feel that requiring everyone to do something with their own body even if they don't agree with it could pave the way for people to accept the loss of other personal freedoms. They feel that it would eventually lead to the development of an authoritative and totalitarian society with a government that dictates every aspect of everyone's everyday lives.

Now imagine that there is a policy already in place. The practice of this policy is an infringement on yours and many other people's rights. The enforcement of this law makes it so you and many others are unable to enjoy the freedoms that certain other people in your society can. This law may have been created and accepted long before you or anyone in your community was born but nonetheless, is something that obstructs your movements, impedes your development or, in some other way, unjustly affects you and the lives of many others. The overall social tolerance for this policy has reached its end. Even people who are not affected by it still disagree with it and also believe it should be changed. However, the lawmakers and enforcers refuse to do away with it. For whatever reason, the people who make the laws still feel as though this policy is fair and necessary. Waiting for these lawmakers to be voted out of office is no longer an option. This policy has taken its toll on you and your community for too long as it is. The time for this policy and social norm to change is now.

Or, perhaps, you, along with a large part of the population are just not satisfied with the direction your country is headed. The overall state of the country is not living up to the expectations that were set for you when you were younger. The principles and beliefs that you developed as a result of these expectations seem to have been compromised over and over again. Your patriotism has been built on traditions and customs that were once a staple in your society but, now seem to be falling to the wayside. Every person from your preferred political party who has been elected to office has let you and your affiliates down in one way or another. You feel that your commitment to the ideals on which your country was built has been betrayed. The more the country changes, the more worried and angrier you get. With an overwhelming urge to return to a time that was glorified for people like you, a time when the country you love exemplified every standard and value that you hold dear, you've faithfully returned to the voting booth, cast your ballot, and have been disappointed to find out that the man you put all of your trust and belief in, did not do for you what he promised he would.

These 4 scenarios are not only possible but, at one point or another, have in fact been a reality in our very own society. Given these 4 scenarios, what is to be done? How do the people make their voices heard? What do the people do when no one will listen? How is the change that people are demanding to become a reality? As it stands, it would seem that there are two different answers to the same question. Which answer you get depends on what which issue you are trying to resolve and what side of that issue you're on.

Dissatisfaction with the state of society is not a new phenomenon. There have always been people who are frustrated or upset with their respective society or the people who run it. Amerikan schools teach children about the so-called Revolutionary War. The perspective from which we're taught places this conflict in the context of triumph. We're taught that throughout the entire colonial era, the colonists were under the oppression of the king of England. People who invaded and infested a land that wasn't theirs, killed off over 75% of the people who that land did belong to and enslaved tens of millions of people to work that land for an ungodly amount of profit were depicted as being oppressed because they had to pay taxes for the profits being generated. When the colonists decided they wanted to break from the restrictive governorship of England and establish their own, they were prepared to go to war for it. And that's precisely what they did. And in fact, took it a step further by making the people they enslaved go to war for them. These colonists were distinctly white, Christian, rich, slave owning men. Their pro-Amerikanism was born in fundamental, conservative protest for the "right" to profit from slave labor without paying taxes on the profits produced by slave labor. To King George III and his loyal subjects, however, these men were villains. They were criminals. Treasonous troublemakers who deserved to be hanged. But the way we're taught about them is in a much different light. We're taught that they were the oppressed underdogs who overcame insurmountable odds and liberated themselves from tyranny. We're taught to view them as heroes.

In the summer of 1963, hundreds of thousands of Black people and their supporters gathered in front of the Washington memorial to push for civil rights legislation. Many speeches were given by some of the Black community's most prominent leaders. This demonstration was highly criticized and discouraged by the country's political leaders, including President Kennedy who professed to be an ally to Black people and their quest for civil rights. Eventually, despite the widespread opposition to it, this demonstration helped to pressure congress into passing the civil rights act of 1964.

The Montgomery bus boycotts that lasted just over a year from 1955 to 1956 in which tens of thousands of Black people refused to ride the bus in protest of the treatment they received and the segregation laws in Montgomery, Alabama. The boycott resulted in the U.S. Supreme Court upholding a decision made earlier by a Montgomery Federal Court which ruled that any law requiring segregation on public transportation was a violation of the constitution. However, white Alabama was largely displeased with the decision and Montgomery bus integration was met with violence. Snipers began shooting into the busses. Black churches and homes were bombed. Eventually, 7 members of the KKK were arrested for the the acts of violence which brought about an effective end to it.

On August 26th, 2016, professional Amerikan football player Colin Kaepernick refused to stand while the pre-game national anthem was playing. Noticed and brought to the attention of the Amerikan public by the media, pictures of Kaepernick sitting while everyone else stood covering their hearts went viral. Choosing later to kneel during the national anthem, Kaepernick continued his silent and peaceful protest of police brutality and racial injustice in Amerika. Eventually, despite his undeniable talent, Kaepernick was effectively barred from playing professional football and ostracized by the league. Not a single shot was fired. Not a single brick was thrown. Not a single shop was burned down. Not a single highway was blocked. Not a single person was late to work. Not a single ambulance was obstructed. Not a single space was unlawfully occupied. Not a single person was inconvenienced due to Kaepernick's protest.

The Chicago Riot of 1919, the Harlem Riots of 1935, 1943, and 1964, the Watts Riot of 1965, the Detroit Riot of 1967, the Los Angeles Riots of 1992, the Minneapolis Riot of 2020, and many others all resulted from the failure of police to recognize Black people as human. In one way or another, the police either directly initiated the murder of a Black person or in some way facilitated or complicit in the murder of a Black person.

That list of riots spans over a century. 100 years of fear, anger, pain, resentment, and distrust from the Black community towards police who to this day, continue to threaten the lives of every single Black person at any given time. A century which, incidentally, is only a small sample of the overall time spent by Black people enduring these conditions. Calls for an end to the murders of Black people by police have been peaceful and violent. Disruptive and civil. Organized and spontaneous. Defiant and compliant. Demonstrated in every conceivable way imaginable because it is an issue that has been minimized, denied, degraded, and ignored. The fact that this same issue has been mobilizing Black people in any and every possible way for at least the past 150 years is evidence that this is a very real, very serious, and very chronic issue that has not only been a threat to the Black community since the advent of police but, is also an issue that no one is willing to address in any kind of institutional context. In the words of Martin Luther King, Jr., "A riot is the language of the unheard".

Between the night of August 11th and the evening of August 12th, 2017, a large coalition of self-identified white supremacists and nationalists gathered in Charlottesville, Virginia to declare unity among all white supremacist organizations on the Amerikan right. Armed with tiki torches, khaki pants, and neo-Nazi haircuts, this public display of bigotry and hatred brought international attention to the genocidal nature of conservatism. With Donald Trump as their champion, mascot, and messiah, the alt-Right, neo-Nazis, neo-Confederates, Klansmen, fascists, and white supremacist militias all gathered to express their disapproval that a statue of the man who led the charge to try and preserve chattel slavery, Robert E. Lee was scheduled to be taken down. In hindsight, it seems as though it was more of a pretext to coalesce their racist brethren and insight violence against any who opposed their mission of bringing classical fascism to the Amerikan political arena. Using tiki torches eerily reminiscent of when Klansmen rode on horseback to burn down houses, the night of August 11th saw these white supremacists marching through the streets of Virginia chanting "white lives matter", "Jews will not replace us", and "Blood and soil" (a neo-Nazi slogan). Attempting to protect what they believed to be a symbol of freedom (a very common misconception in Amerika) counter-protesters locked arms around a statue of Thomas Jefferson where the white supremacist march was heading. Upon their arrival, the white supremacists surrounded the counter-protesters and as a brawl ensued, they began throwing their torches amid the melee.

Around 8 a.m. on August 12th, both protesters, this time armed with semiautomatic rifles, and counter-protesters, some also armed, began to gather in anticipation of the white supremacist rally scheduled to start at noon and go till 5 p.m. Again, the racist protesters, with posts on their website threatening to burn down a synagogue, chanted slogans calling for violence and oppression to anyone who was not a white, heterosexual male. In response to the violence called for by the white supremacists, counter-protesters began to shout their own slogans including "punch a Nazi" and "kill all Nazis". Cornell West, who had organized a small group of peaceful counter protesters, mentioned that if it weren't not for the militant counter-protesters coming to their defense, he and his group "would have been crushed like cockroaches". Later, Richard Preston who is the self-proclaimed Imperial Wizard of the Confederate White Knights of the KKK, was caught on video shooting a gun at Black counter-protester Corey Long who was armed with aerosol can and a lighter. The rally had been declared unlawful assembly and Riot police cleared the scene. After the aborted rally while white supremacists were gathering in a nearby park, Alex Fields drove his car into a crowd of counter-protesters killing Heather Heyer and injuring 35 others.

On January 6, 2021, an unruly mob of Trump supporters swarmed the nation's Capitol to express their disapproval and try to forcibly over-turn the results of the election that Trump had just lost. As it turns out, this mob formed at the suggestion of Trump himself who, most likely due to his spoiled upbringing coupled with his delusions of grandeur, being unable to take loss graciously, or even realize his own incompetence, made an abundance of false claims that the election was rigged against him and urged his followers to "fight like hell". Whether or not the elec-tion was actually rigged is irrelevant considering that the people who were at the Capitol to lay siege to it were the same people who, just 4 years earlier, told every other Amerikan dismayed by Trump's initial elec-tion in 2016 that they should just accept it. Oh, the hypocrisy! Neverthe-less, his ever-faithful legion of dumb hung onto and fell for his every word. The stage was set for an unnecessary, self-righteous and overall delu-sional uprising at the United States Capitol. Amid the self-delusional in-dignation, rioters assaulted police, destroyed property, and occupied the Capitol for several hours. Breaching the perimeters set by police, they stormed the building, vandalized, looted, and attempted to locate law makers in order to capture and harm them. Gallows had even been erected as the threats to hang Vice President Mike Pence who had re-jected Trump's claims grew more and more serious. Pipe bombs and Mol-otov cocktails were also found in vehicles and at the RNC headquarters.

During the entire ordeal, many people were injured including 138 police officers, 5 rioters who were hospitalized and one woman who was fatally shot during the siege. Trump, still holding the presidential title for another 2 weeks before his successor was set to officially take over, refused to call in the national guard. However, later that afternoon, in a Twitter video, Trump maintained the fraudulent nature of the election but did instruct his mob to go home.

All of these different situations raise a number of points when compared with each other. First, it is neither the opposition nor the fence rider's place to question the methods used by those who intend to cast off the weight of oppression. Those who side with the abuse of power that is being challenged are in no position to dictate how that challenge is to be pursued. Furthermore, those who would rather bury their heads in the sand or refuse to pick a side cannot, with any credibility, tell those who have resolved to stand firm how to make their stand. Those who say it should not be done must not interrupt those who are doing it.

Second, as John F. Kennedy said, "those who make peaceful revolution impossible will make violent revolution inevitable." For every public injustice, there is a public response. The frequency and lengthy recurrence of the murder of Black people with complete impunity at the hands of police has left it necessary for the public response to increase in severity. When cries and pleas for both justice and peace continue to fall on willfully deaf ears, those with the deaf ears are making peaceful resolve impossible. In such a case, those who are asking for peace and justice are left with no choice but to turn those demands that get louder and louder.

Third, it would seem that civil disturbance on both sides is never completely out of the question. What is in question, however, is both what the motivation as well as the validity of that motivation for civil disturbance on each side is. On one side, there apparently is a specific intent to commit physical violence. To purposely target, threaten the safety of and inflict unprovoked harm upon another person's body. This intent was used a means to achieve a particular goal that is inconsistent with the pursuit of justice considering no injustice had been committed. Unproven claims of election fraud and tearing down monuments to racism are decidedly not acts of injustice. The desire and intent to commit any violence against people you consider to be inferior is indeed injustice. But not against those who intend to commit the violence.

On the other side, the civil disturbance cannot be summed up so simply as it cannot be placed into the context of an isolated incident.

Firstly, the civil unrest committed by those who are responding to centuries of patternized violence committed against them was not the first course of action they took to subdue that violence. But the peaceful protests, sit-ins, and marches were all met with physical violence. And it was met with physical violence by those whose violence was being protested. It was only the repeated refusal to remove the violence committed against them that brought about the civil unrest. Secondly, the right to self-defense is a constitutionally protected right. If the violence that is ravaging a particular community continues without a satisfactory resolution to eliminate that violence by those in power, then what are the people who suffer from the violence supposed to do? Now, ask yourself, what are the people who suffer from the violence supposed to do when it is the people in power who are committing the violence? As Walter Rodney said, "By what standard of morality can the violence used by a slave to break his chains be considered the same as the violence of a slave master?" The violence of those who are provoked cannot be considered the same as the violence of those who provoke. The violence of those who are provoked would not have occurred if those who provoke hadn't been violent first. The police murder of Black people has been a provocation in that community for centuries. And it is a provocation that was not first answered with civil disturbances and uprisings. However, if it were, Black people would still have been well within their human rights to do so given the natural law of self-defense. If you don't believe that Black people are just as entitled to the right of self-defense against any and every threat to their lives as white people, then you don't believe Black people are humans.

The stark differences in these comparisons raises another very pertinent question. Just what is it that qualifies as violence? Violence comes in 4 basic forms. Physical, sexual, emotional, and psychological. When white supremacists are marching through the streets shouting chants that have traditionally been used to signify both their feelings of superiority as well as their intent to assert and enforce those feelings, it is through a threat of violence. The threat of physical violence is itself psychological violence. The attempt to assert and act on feelings of superiority is an implicit threat of subjugation. This also is psychological violence and implies the probability of physical violence in order to enforce the subjugation. When counter-protesters are responding to this violence with a refusal to take it passively, it is unacceptable and inaccurate to measure the response of counter-protesters with the same yardstick of violence as is used to measure the threat of violence and subjugation by white supremacists. The intent to punch a Nazi in the face is a response to the presence of Nazis, and all white supremacists alike, which is already inherently violent given the entire reason for a Nazi's existence. The failure to meet the presence of white supremacists with force is what creates a safe place for them to thrive and spread their ideology, which is already violent.

When a dimly lit mob of Trump supporters are storming the U.S. Capitol because they believe that election fraud stole the presidency from their even dimmer messiah, we have to be willing to separate the violent from the extreme. Just because it's extreme doesn't mean it's violent. We also have to be willing to separate the misguided from the violent. Just because they were duped into being extreme doesn't mean they committed violence. However, the absence of violence from some does not mean the absence of violence from all. With all of that said, it's important to be able to identify the violence that did occur. All of it. Did those who vandalized and looted the building commit violence? Well, was anyone hurt by the vandalism and looting? The answer to that is no. The acts of vandalism and looting do not themselves threaten or remove entirely the safety and security of anyone's immediate well-being. Being inconvenienced is not the same as being violated. However, the people that sustained physical injuries during the ordeal were violated. They did have violence committed against them. Therefore, the people who stormed the Capitol and caused the injuries were indeed violent. Moreover, since the threat of physical violence is itself psychological violence, then erecting Gallows with the threat to hang the vice president is also violence.

Conversely, when a Black person is murdered by police for the hundredth time in one year, not only is the presence of violence obvious but, also, so too is it obvious who the violence is targeting. When this violence continues to go unaddressed, unacknowledged, and unrectified, the response to this violence will inevitably, and rightly, grow more and more intense. And, when the intensity of that response reaches the point of vandalism and looting, two things become apparent. First, it was the lack of accountability and the continued negligence to remedy the violence that increased the anger to it. It is the anger over the failure to remove the violence that necessitated the burning, vandalism, and looting. Second, equating the value of vandalism, burning, destruction and looting of inanimate buildings and material objects with the value of a Black life lost at the hands of murderous racists is inaccurate, degrading, and offensive. The only reason you're able to get so upset at the destruction and looting of buildings in response to the continued murder of Black life is because you don't consider Black lives to be worth more than buildings and commodities.

Lastly, even when Black people do protest peacefully, there is still more public outcry at their peaceful tactics of protest than there is at the violent tactics of genocidal white supremacists and the band of MAGA maniacs pathetic excuse for an insurrection. The country gets more upset at blocked highways and kneeling during a song than they do about the loss of innocent lives and the looming threat of Nazism marching down the streets. Coming up with inapplicable and far-fetched arguments for not blocking highways or kneeling during the national anthem seems more important to the vast majority of the country than demanding an end to police violence in the Black community. Even though it's perfectly common for ambulances to get stuck in traffic and is standard practice for dispatch to send another unit when this happens, most of the Amerikan population would rather worry about a hypothetical emergency than an actual victim. You got to wonder if people feel the same way when these highways are closed by construction workers. Rather than considering that ambulance dispatchers' routinely use computer aided dispatch that maps out alternate routes to them so that they can convey those routes to the drivers in the event of construction closure of highways, the country would rather conjure up any scenario that could invalidate a protest in order to keep from admitting that there is a serious problem which makes the protest necessary.

The arrogance of white people bred by centuries of white supremacy has made us so narcissistic that any issue which doesn't center us as the focus is either invalid or we have to go and make it about us. Somehow, kneeling during the national anthem became disrespectful to military service members when the issue at hand had absolutely nothing to do with them whatsoever. So, we need to admit the fact that our problem really has nothing to do with the way they protest and everything to do with why they protest. Either we believe in the cause that Black lives do, in fact, matter and stop critiquing the way they speak out or we need to admit that we think Black people should suffer the murderous police and the threat of genocidal white supremacists in silence.

The hypocrisy that is so evident in these arguments is a testament to the dangers of failing to think critically. This hypocrisy indicates just how easy it is to lead people off a cliff. This hypocrisy signifies how gullible people become when they choose to listen to their egos over their conscience. And it shows just how arrogant we are. Hypocrisy is the prime example of stupidity. It is the perfect demonstration of idiocy combined with egotism. Because although you have to be stupid to be a bigot. Being a bigot makes you even stupider. The fact is, hypocrisy or not, there will never be form of protest that is acceptable to people who don't want things to change. And the only people who don't want things to change are the people that benefit from the way things are.

Chapter 19
White Arrogance

In the interest of mutual understanding, it is probably a good idea to offer some clarity on a few of the terms that aren't exactly everyday language but do help to gain insight into the topic. I apologize if it comes across as patronizing. I'm just trying to make this as widely accessible as possible. This chapter uses terms like "systems of oppression", "systems of dominance", "social order", social arrangement", "hierarchical order", and many others that are similar. A system of oppression or dominance can basically be summed up as any system that a society uses as its standard function that is inherently oppressive. For instance, capitalism is inherently oppressive by nature because it forces people into positions that prevent them from determining their own destiny. We do not get a say in what our pay is, we do not get a say in what our schedule is, we do not get a say in what is done with the products we make, we do not get a say in where and how the profits that are received from what we produce are allocated, etc. Furthermore, capitalism allows the bosses to exploit the people who do the work. If the value of a product comes from the work that it takes to make it and that value determines the price that it is sold for, then the profit that is received from selling said product rightfully belongs to the people who directly made the product. Since, that profit does not go to the people who made it, capitalism is exploiting the workers by taking the money that should go to them and giving it to the bosses. Lastly, the way capitalism applies to society requires the average worker to rent out his labor for a wage in order to survive. Therefore, capitalism can be categorized as a system of dominance.

Social order just means the way that society is arranged. If we pan out and look at society in everyday life, we can see that it operates according to specific arrangements. For instance, children going to school is a part of the social arrangement, people going to work so a part of the social arrangement, paying rent and mortgages is a part of the social arrangement. The laws, the way politics are practiced, the way crime is dealt with, all of these are a part of the social arrangement or social order. Hierarchical merely refers to any situation or circumstance that is arranged from top to bottom. Such arrangements can be seen in the workplace. There's the owner (top), the district manager (lower), the store manager (lower), the supervisor (lower), and the employee (bottom). This arrangement can also be seen in the classroom, in the court room and so on. With all of that said, let's continue.

As previously mentioned, Dr. Martin Luther King, Jr. once remarked, "Whites, it must be frankly said, are not putting in a similar mass effort to reeducate themselves out of their racial ignorance. It is an aspect of their sense of superiority that the white people of Ameri[k]a believe they have little to learn." This quotation perfectly expresses the arrogance exemplified by most white people in Amerika when confronted about the systems of oppression that were constructed to benefit our ancestors as well as are currently maintained to benefit us either through tacit complicity or by the arrogance that has grown out of centuries of white domination.

Even before this country's official inception, the race of white people who reside within the United States borders have been favored by its racial caste system that placed us above all others in the United States's social, economic, and political arrangements. Although not all white people actively occupy the highest status in the hierarchy, collectively we do all make up the upper social and economic statuses that hang over the heads of all people of color. The foundations on which this country was built have been orientated to protect and procure the prosperity and freedom of wealthy white men. Initially, these foundations were built at the expense of everyone who was not a wealthy male, white or otherwise. However, because of the racial caste system that was created by these men with the purpose of ensuring that these foundations remained in their favor, some of the privileges that were unintentionally produced would inevitably trickle down to other, less wealthy, and also less male people simply because we all shared the same white skin tone. These privileges helped to further solidify the sense of superiority that white people were conditioned to feel towards people of color.

As a whole, when a people spend centuries participating in the upper echelons of any hierarchical order, there tends to be some mentalities that will inevitably arise and become adopted by those who occupy this status. Over time, these mentalities become normalized in the minds of those who adopt them and then handed down from generation to generation through family and social conditioning. These mentalities are rooted in the effect that the status itself has on the egos of those who occupy it. When society is constructed in a top – down fashion, those who reside at the top parts - or upper statuses - are generally unaware of the everyday experiences, as well as how different those experiences are from their own, of the people in the lower statuses. And because we live in a very divided, cellular society, it is very unlikely that we are able to recognize the inequalities and differences of the struggles between those at the top and those at the bottom. This does not mean that those who are at the top don't have any struggles. It means that those struggles are vastly different because they are relative to status. The lower the status, the more difficult the struggles. The struggles become more difficult simply because access to resources becomes more and more limited the lower the status goes. Therefore, since capitalism is where racism gets its power, and capitalism is also what causes poverty, then the struggles of those at the bottom become compounded due to the combination of hardships.

As a result of being in the upper racial statuses of society we are not faced with the same struggles as those at the bottom. Since we are not faced with those struggles, we often fail to account for them or deny they exist altogether. This is where and when we start to develop a sense of entitlement, authority, defensiveness, and superiority. These mentalities form in the minds of those who are endowed with privileges and liberties that are almost exclusive to their status, and of which they are generally unaware. Said mentalities are combined into, and expressed as, arrogance. Because our current society was built with racism determined by skin color, the arrogance that is formed and expressed is also based on skin color. Ergo, white arrogance.

White arrogance stems from the inevitable establishment of three particular mind sets that are developed by those of us who occupy the top of the hierarchical paradigm. These three particular mentalities are naturally virulent and destructive due to our refusal to recognize them. Our failure to recognize them comes from the fear of losing our superior social position. In order to secure our placement in the superior social position, we develop these attitudes as defense mechanisms.

The first mentality is one in which any challenge to our supposed superiority is met with derision, condescension, and minimizing or flat-out rejection of alternative perspectives. Moreover, those of us who are in the upper racial social position will have a sense of superiority that will also necessarily generate a sense of entitlement to authority. As such we feel justified in asserting any authoritative measure with which to maintain our status and sense of superiority.

The second mentality that can be expected to arise in the minds of those at the top of the hierarchy is one in which the ego plays a central role. Simply stated, the longer one is at the top, the more inflated the ego becomes. Consequently, the more inflated an ego becomes, the more sensitive the ego gets. And, subsequently, the more sensitive an ego gets, the more attention it demands.

In this case, any social movement, campaign, or attempt at mass cognitive redirection that does not directly focus its attention on those who feel entitled to it is thereby vilified or invalidated. Basically, because society was set up to favor and cater to our white skin tone, we feel justified in the arrogance we develop. When that arrogance is challenged with facts or is not actively being gratified, we will take any measure we can think of to invalidate or demonize whatever it is that is threatening the comfort of our arrogance. Ironically, despite the threat that the current social order poses to those who do not directly benefit from it, any suggestion of an alternative social paradigm to the status quo is seen as a very real threat to those who occupy the upper statuses. The thought of losing the validation that comes from being the center of attention and constantly glorified is perceived as a threat of oppression. The irony that lies behind this fear of an upset social order is the lack of realization to the oppressive nature of the current order that favors us. The failure to recognize the current social order as oppressive to others while fearing any shift in the dynamic of that social order due to a fear of being oppressed by it is necessarily symptomatic of the internally focused, egocentric attitude developed by a people who have intergenerationally occupied the top of the aforementioned hierarchical order. Again, when attention is not focused directly on those who are so used to receiving it, there tends to be an outward display of emotion that impedes any chance for social progress.

A further aspect of the second mentality is one in which the attempts to point out our more obscured racist proclivities and the ideology we uphold to maintain structural racism is expected to be met with outward hostility and offense. Ostensibly, white people are unable to separate the white supremacist conditioning we've unwittingly been subjected to from the voluntary choices in morality that we make. The inability or unwillingness to separate the two stems from the role that society plays in catering to our egos. Because everything in society is geared towards inflating our sense of superiority, we automatically take every indictment personally, rather than objectively analyzing the content of the indictment through a sociopolitical lens. We are unable to separate our personal feelings from objective reality because of the investment our egos have in being the center of attention. If the center of attention shines a less than favorable light on our ego, we automatically resort to defensive behaviors that serve to protect an ego that has been shaped and molded by white supremacist conditioning. The demonstrable hostility, passive-aggressive commentary, and other behaviors can be indicative of an egotistical investment in our own reality. This investment proceeds from a Eurocentric conditioning that the social structures, political institutions, economic systems, and contemporary religious dynamics under which society as a whole function are of a superior nature to any and all alternatives. Because of the privileges afforded to those of us with European roots by these social, political, economic, and religious dynamics, our egos become invested in their continuity. Ergo, everything from pop culture to media, to mainstream political rhetoric to black history - yes, even black history - is centered around the glorification and appeasement of white people. Thus, we are unable to objectively evaluate our own mentalities that are tied to the maintenance of our egos because to do so would be a threat to their very selves.

The third mentality that can be observed is simply known as whitesplaining. Whitesplaining is when white people become so arrogant that we feel it is our place to both explain oppressed people's oppression to them as well as instruct them on how to get out from under that oppression. This is a presumptuous action stemming from the often subconscious notion that Black people are unable to interpret, analyze, and articulate their own experiences and circumstances. Whitesplaining is the final stage in the development of white arrogance. Our arrogance reaches full maturity when we feel qualified to explain issues we have never and will never experience to those who face them every day.

All Lives Matter, Blue Lives Matter, Tomi Lahren, Ben Shapiro and cultural appropriation are perfect examples of white arrogance. With white arrogance, behaviors such as stonewalling, combativeness, defensiveness, and denial are driven by an undeserved sense of superiority and obsession with being the center of attention. For the past 450 years, everything in the U.S. has been for or about white people. Finally, when the spotlight is not on us, or shines a less than favorable light on our historical and modern development, we resort to tactics that obstruct a collective focus on the real issue and prevent tangible resolve. The superlative nature of the hierarchical positions that we occupy have dictated the direction of social attention towards us. This acute societal focus on our position has effectively gone to our heads. We feel that we have nothing to learn. We're convinced that our position in history is due to our superior intellect and knowledge. When that intellect and attention is challenged, we exhibit the behaviors that we feel will best serve to protect our current social position.

Any socially conscious person with a shred of motivation to change the miserable conditions in which oppressed people, most notably Black and Native people, are forced to live, have more than likely had a discussion with at least one socially unaware white person regarding the maintenance and support that we as white people lend to institutional racism. More often than not, these conversations culminate into a verbal battle initiated by a combative, willfully ignorant white person who refuses to accept any vestige of truth to the narrative that challenges their current level of social comfort. The behaviors and dispositions that tend to accompany these conflicts can be characterized, by the arguer's strong propensity towards either attempted correction or accusations of reverse racism. White people must come to terms with the fact that there is a lot we can learn from Black, Brown, and Native people if we could only just shut up, listen, and accept the fact that we will never know what it is like to live in a world that is constantly targeting us while at the same time telling us we're crazy when we speak up about it.

Chapter 20
Tacit Complicity: Non-Racist vs Anti-Racist

Archbishop Desmond Tutu once said that "If you choose to remain silent in times of oppression, you have chosen the side of the oppressor". The phenomenon known as tacit complicity is one of the most common ways that otherwise well-intentioned white people still manage to be racist. Approaching social ills such as racism with the attitude that we are not responsible for it because we ourselves are not inflicting it, on the contrary, makes us responsible for its existence. Even if we never say or do or think anything racist in our whole lives, we can still be racist. However, as we've discussed throughout the book, in a white supremacist society such as ours, that is impossible to do without consciously working at it. By failing to openly and unapologetically challenge racism when we witness it - no matter how inadvertent or subtle it may be - as well as actively working to dismantle the social, economic, and political systems that were built with it, while continuously working to challenge any racist beliefs or attitudes we ourselves hold, we are just as guilty of racism as the KKK. If we allow racism to go unchallenged it means we allow racism. Giving racism a safe place to exist and grow makes us guilty of racism.

Racism is virulent. It's cancerous. If we do not fight it, it will continue to grow and destroy. If an oncology doctor allows a tumor to grow without doing everything in their power to stop it, then they are just as responsible for the patient's death as the cancer itself. White people created racism. This is not to say that we created prejudice or discrimination. Those existed long before racism. But we did organize prejudice and discrimination with the power to enforce it based on skin color. This is what makes us the creators of racism. As such, it is our responsibility to dismantle it. Despite all the selfish and socially divisive rhetoric to the contrary, to be a human being means that we are, in fact, responsible for the decisions our ancestors made. Just as our children will be responsible for the decisions that we make. However, as white people we are especially responsible because we still benefit from the decisions that our ancestors made to create and institute the social, economic, and political systems which we still operate as a society under to this day. To be tacit, idle, inactive, is to be complicit in the existence and assertion of racism. As the venerable and incomparable Angela Davis said "it is no longer enough to not be racist. It is time to be anti-racist". In fact, the only way to not be racist is to be anti-racist. It is no longer enough to reject the practice of racism in our personal lives and think that this is sufficient enough to absolve us of racism. In order to not be racist, we must be actively fighting it in some way, shape, or form. We must be anti-racist to qualify as not racist. And even then, chances are, we still hold some subliminal racist attitudes or beliefs.

To be anti-racist is to consciously and conscientiously fight racism wherever and whenever we are in its presence. Yes, this means at all times. If not in one way, then in another. If not in others, then in ourselves. We need to understand that racism is a two-way street. At any and all given times, white people are either fighting racism or perpetuating it. If we are not actively and consciously fighting racism, then we are passively and tacitly perpetuating it by simply allowing it to happen.

The fight against racism must be as dynamic and flexible as racism itself. However, let us also understand that the sheer nature of racism's durability demands that our fight against it be sustainable and uncompromising enough to defeat it completely. This may seem contradictory however, what this means is that we must be willing to fight racism at any and all times while simultaneously being willing to accept that our understanding of racism can always be deeper. We must be willing to learn as we fight.

Both fighting racism and perpetuating it occur on the same two fronts. The first is socially. There are so many different ways that racism can arise in our everyday lives. Any one of the topics in the previous chapters is almost certain to confront us on a daily basis through our friends, family, peers, colleagues, co-workers, etc. We must be vigilant in recognizing them when they do arise because they won't always be so obvious even with our newfound perspective on racism. We must also understand that the institutions of education, prison, police, and the medical industry as they are practiced in the western world, are all inherently racist as well. It is just as imperative for us to fight to dismantle these institutions in order to create new ones that actually address the needs that are failing to be met by the old ones. The institutions of education, prisons, police, and the medical industry cannot meet the needs of a society that is healthy, equal, substantial and free. The police do not serve and protect. Prisons do not rehabilitate. Education does not educate. The medical industry does not cure. All of these institutions are implemented and practiced in society at the expense of Black people and people of color. They must also not go unchallenged.

The second front on which racism must be fought is personally. As a whole, white people are more concerned with not being called racist than we are with not being racist. We will do anything to keep from being called racist except not be racist. If we actually cared about not being racist as much as we care about not being called racist, we would do more to educate ourselves on racism and why it is that white people don't get to determine what is and isn't racist. We must have the courage and humility to challenge our current way of thinking. We need to make an objective analysis on what our attitudes and beliefs are regarding issues that are caused by us but do not affect us. We have to be brave enough and honest enough to challenge our own thought processes. We must commit to eradicating ideas and beliefs that have the underlying implications of subjugating and degrading others. We have got to commit to changing our attitudes toward racism if they do not serve to further our understanding and recognition of it. We have to understand that it is a privilege that we only have to learn about racism instead of experience it. Then we have to continue to learn about it. We have to educate ourselves and each other on it. Because until no white people are racist, all white people are racist.